AMERICAN EDUCATION

Its Men,

Ideas,

and

Institutions

Advisory Editor

Lawrence A. Cremin
Frederick A. P. Barnard Professor of Education
Teachers College, Columbia University

AMERICAN EDUCATION: *Its Men, Ideas, and Institutions*
presents selected works of thought and scholarship that have
long been out of print or otherwise unavailable. Inevitably, such
works will include particular ideas and doctrines that have been
outmoded or superseded by more recent research. Nevertheless,
all retain their place in the literature, having influenced educational thought and practice in their own time and having provided
the basis for subsequent scholarship.

PROGRESSIVE EDUCATION AT THE CROSSROADS

BY

BOYD H. BODE

ARNO PRESS & THE NEW YORK TIMES

*New York * 1971*

Reprint Edition 1971 by Arno Press Inc.

Reprinted from a copy in
  The Newark Public Library

American Education:
  Its Men, Ideas, and Institutions - Series II
ISBN for complete set: 0-405-03600-0
See last pages of this volume for titles.

Manufactured in the United States of America

Library of Congress Cataloging in Publication Data

Bode, Boyd Henry, 1873-1953.
    Progressive education at the crossroads.
    (American education: its men, ideas, and
institutions. Series II)
    1. Education--Experimental methods.
2. Educational psychology. I. Title.
II. Series.
LB875.B518 1971   370.1   71-165707
ISBN 0-405-03696-5

PROGRESSIVE EDUCATION AT THE CROSSROADS

BY

BOYD H. BODE
Ohio State University

NEWSON & COMPANY
NEW YORK *and* CHICAGO

Other Books by BOYD H. BODE

(ISSUED BY VARIOUS PUBLISHERS)

An Outline of Logic (1910)

Fundamentals in Education (1922)

Modern Educational Theories (1927)

Conflicting Psychologies of Learning (1929)

Democracy as a Way of Life (1937)

[2]

PREFACE

As a national organization progressive education is now twenty years old. The beginnings of the movement date back much farther. While the movement has never been sharply defined, its most prominent connotation has been that of "child-centeredness," in the sense that it has been guided largely by such concepts as "interest," "freedom," and "self-activity." In its psychology progressive education has leaned towards the point of view indicated, somewhat vaguely, by the phrase, "learning by doing." In its social philosophy it has stressed the worth of the individual, or respect for personality, and the importance of superseding habits of competition with habits of co-operation.

It can hardly be denied that the progressive movement has contributed much of great and lasting value to American education. As was perhaps to be expected, it has also led to various aberrations and errors. The psychological and philosophical implications of the movement were never widely understood, and, consequently, a certain amount of misinterpretation was inevitable. Such misinterpretation is bound to limit the influence of the movement and to retard its development. This is particularly true at the present time when the world is disposed to look more and more to education as a means of promoting the coming of a better social order.

The purpose of this little book is to contribute to a better understanding of the philosophy in which the progressive movement must find its justification and by which it must be tested. This philosophy derives its content from the implications contained in the emphasis which is placed on "respect for personality" and "maximum development" by the progressive movement. It has generally been taken for granted that respect for personality and maximum development can be achieved by the simple process of becoming emancipated from the formalism of traditional education and by improving the conditions of learning. This shortsighted view inevitably leads to aberrations and frustration.

World events during recent years are serving grim notice that education must be based on a philosophy of social organization if it is to be a worthy occupation for grownups. By implication the insistence on respect for personality and maximum development is a fighting doctrine. It commits the progressive movement to a point of view which, in ancient phrase, makes man the measure of things. Progressive education must either become a challenge to all the basic beliefs and attitudes which have been dominant for so long in every important domain of human interest, or else retreat to the nursery. If progressive education is to fulfil its promise, it must become consciously representative of a distinctive way of life.

Acknowledgments are due to the following periodicals: *Progressive Education, The Peabody Reflector, The New Republic,* and *Education.* These journals have graciously granted permission to use material which had previously been published by them.

BOYD H. BODE

COLUMBUS, OHIO
March 9, 1938

CONTENTS

PROGRESSIVE EDUCATION AT THE CROSSROADS

CHAPTER I

PROGRESSIVE EDUCATION AND DEMOCRACY

The strongest and most evangelistic movement in American education at the present time is the movement known as progressive education. A visitor to our schools ordinarily has no difficulty in recognizing a so-called progressive school. He can usually tell the difference the moment he opens the door. The progressive school cultivates an atmosphere of activity and freedom which is all its own. In academic language, the progressive school is a place where children go, not primarily to learn, but to carry on a way of life.

THE PROGRESSIVES' PARADOX

In spite of this distinctiveness, however, our visitor, if he is a reflective person, is likely to have peculiar difficulty in defining a progressive school. Any trait or aspect which he may select as a distinguish-

9

ing characteristic presently turns out to have significant limitations. In other words, we seem to encounter a variety of contradictions when we try to state the qualities of such a school.

It emphasizes freedom, yet it also attaches major importance to guidance and direction. It plays up method, but it is also critical of the content of the more conventional curriculum. It places the individual at the center of the stage; yet it perpetually criticizes the competitive character of the present social order, which indicates that it rejects the philosophy of individualism. It insists that intelligence must be permitted to operate freely; yet it seldom alarms its constituents, who, in the case of private schools, are generally the more prosperous element in society. It commonly regards the college as the citadel of its enemy; yet its chief business is often preparation for college. It holds that learning takes place through doing; yet physical activity tapers off sharply as we go up the educational scale. To the earnest observer all this is very confusing.

These real or apparent contradictions naturally invite the conclusion that the progressive movement draws its chief inspiration from a certain sentimentality about children. This sentimentality, so it appears, leads to a lot of unedifying

fussiness, which is camouflaged as "respect for personality," but is not intended to be really subversive.
There is no intention of changing the established
values of society beyond the point of spreading more
sweetness and light. With respect to these values
the teachers in our progressive schools are frequently
as conventional as the buttons on the sleeve of a
man's coat.

A New Organizing Principle

Such a conclusion, however, would be a bit too
simple. The continuing vitality of the progressive
movement is evidence that it is based on something
of larger significance. The emphasis of progressive
education on the individual, on the sinfulness of
"imposition," and on the necessity of securing free
play for intelligence, whether rightly or wrongly applied, is a reflection of the growing demand, outside
of the school, for recognition of the common man.
Similarly the confusion in progressive education is
a reflection of the confusion in the outside world
resulting from this demand.

We are gradually discovering that the admission
of the common man to the status of full recognition
means more than an extension of privilege. It is

not on a par, for example, with opening the doors of an art gallery to all comers, instead of merely to the chosen few. In its application to industry this recognition obviously means an extensive revision of our conception of property rights and of the function of government. As applied to organized religion it means a shift of emphasis from eternal salvation to progress through social control. In relation to the values of scholarship and esthetic appreciation it means a transformation of these values so that they will not remain a detached occupation for a leisure class and for specialists, but will become incorporated in the affairs of everyday experience. In brief, the recognition of the common man—which is what we call democracy—introduces a point of view which is so far-reaching in its implications as to make democracy a distinctive and competing way of life.

Unless progressive education is content to be simply a method which is available to any teacher and for any purpose, it had better play out its string and become the exponent of that specific way of life for which the name "democracy" is perhaps as good as any. The refusal to take this step would leave progressive education with no guiding principle except random interests and hypothetical needs, and so would justify most of the hard things that have been said about it by its critics. On the other hand, taking this step means that the question of reorganizing or reinterpreting the established values and institutions of our civilization must receive major attention. These values took their character and form in large part at a time when the common man had not yet secured a prominent place in the picture. As was intimated a moment ago, there is considerable ground for the suspicion that our concern for the common man will evaporate into idle words and sentiments, unless we gain some perception of what is required to give the common man his proper share in our social and cultural heritage. To leave our conception of this heritage unchanged means that in our attempts to "socialize" the school population we are really practicing "imposition" on the sly.

In a word, the rise of the common man is the disturbing factor, both on the social and on the educational level. As long as he remained submerged, the situation was comparatively simple. It was commonly taken for granted that the higher cultural values were not for him. It was even supposed that he was too earth-earthy to appreciate them. This supposition was refuted as he gained wider opportunities, but it also appears that his scale of values is somewhat different from that of the aristocratic class by which he was ruled so long in the past. This difference is making itself felt in certain areas, such as industrial relations and organized religion, although it is not any too clear as yet just what kind of reorganization in ideals and practice is required in these areas by the application of the principle of democracy. What reorganization the principle of democracy calls for in the field of education is perhaps even more obscure. This problem must be faced, however, if we are to arrive at a significant and defensible conception of the meaning of the progressive movement in education.

THE COMMON MAN AND HIGHER EDUCATION

Perhaps the simplest approach to this whole question can be made by taking a glance at the development of higher education in this country. There was no assurance that the common man would concern himself seriously about the fruits of scholarship and culture, which had been withheld from him so long. In the words of the French writer and traveler, de Tocqueville, written less than a century ago: "It must be confessed that among the civilized peoples of our age there are few in which the

highest sciences have made so little progress as in
the United States. . . . The future will prove
whether the passion for profound knowledge, so
rare, and so fruitful, can be born and developed as
readily in democratic societies as in aristocracies."

De Tocqueville's comment was pertinent and dis-
passionate and justified by the facts. With respect
to higher education, facilities for advanced study
were then almost completely lacking in this country. To cultivate "the passion for profound knowledge" students had to go abroad. Degrees from
foreign universities were recognized as an almost
indispensable certificate of scholarship. In all the
"highest sciences" and arts we leaned heavily on
Europe, thus giving color to the suspicion that a
democracy is incapable of producing worthy fruits
of its own.

This view of the matter was readily accepted by
other European writers and travelers, who were less
sympathetic than de Tocqueville with the experi-
ment in democracy on these shores. Posing as high
priests of culture they took pains to remind us in
detail of our deficiencies. This seemed to give them
considerable satisfaction and presumably did us no
harm. As far as higher learning is concerned, however, the opportunity for invidious comparisons did

not last very long. When the Johns Hopkins University led the way, in the 'seventies, in emphasizing graduate work, other institutions speedily followed, with the result that American universities are now competing with old-world institutions on their own terms and in various fields are leading the way.

Perhaps the most striking development in this connection is that which took place in our state universities. In spite of their dependence on public opinion and public appropriations, the more important of these institutions found it possible to advance to a front rank in the cultivation of scholarship and cultural interests. We were presented with the unprecedented spectacle of legislatures composed largely of farmers and small business men appropriating large sums for the promotion of scientific studies ranging all the way from the *mores* and speech habits of primitive peoples to the composition of heavenly bodies so remote as to be invisible to the naked eye. Let me remark in passing that while I have seen this happen over and over again, I still have moments when it seems quite incredible. There is perhaps no more convincing evidence to be had anywhere that our democracy, in spite of all its crudities, has at its core an idealism that is both magnificent and indestructible. As Lord Bryce once said: "There is nothing of which Americans boast less and of which they have more reason to be proud than their universities."

It appears, then, that the question whether "the passion for profound knowledge" can flourish as well in a democracy as in an aristocracy may be regarded as settled. To put it in its lowest terms, our institutions of higher learning have their full quota of men who regard their respective subjects as the supreme achievement of civilization, and whose highest expression of broadmindedness consists in identifying the university with the universe. In the light of this development we are tempted to say that the capacity of the common man to appreciate cultural values was seriously underrated, and to let it go at that.

As was suggested previously, however, there is reason to suspect that the appreciation of the cultural values which we have transplanted with so much apparent success into our civilization is not quite the same thing with us as in the Old World. In the language of evolution, the differences in environment seem to make for a variation from type.

The difference is perhaps most easily indicated by the difference in popular attitude, here and abroad, toward the professor, who is presumably the embodiment or symbol of these cultural values. In the Old World the professor is generally regarded with profound respect. Pre-war Germany was once referred to by Lord Palmerston as "the land of the damned professor." Here we tend to distinguish sharply between faith in education and faith in professors. We have an abiding faith in education; and it may be added that this faith is not merely faith in its utilitarian value. As evidence we may point to the fact that the sporadic attempts to make secondary education consist, for most pupils, in vocational preparation have never made much headway. But the professor, who, after all, does the heavy work in education and who presumably should be regarded as an exemplification of what we mean by education, occupies an equivocal status. We distrust him. It was this distrust which the opponents of the New Deal sought to exploit by their constant harping on the "brain trust" and by their ingenious cartoons of unlovely pedagogs arrayed in cap and gown. The common man as a class is certainly not lacking in the recognition that there are cultural values, but at his profane touch these values seem to have been transmuted into something else.

Somewhere along the line there is a parting of the ways; and to discover just where and how the ways diverge is of essential importance if we are to determine the meaning of democracy as applied to education.

Cleavage between Intellectual and Practical

In approaching this problem we may recall de Tocqueville's reminder that "the passion for profound knowledge" was born and developed in the aristocracies of the past, which means that it took on a distinctive quality. Historical aristocracy maintained a cleavage between the cultural and the vocational, between the intellectual and the practical, between the quest for truth and art for their own sake and the recognition of their social significance and responsibility. This cleavage was, of course, a reflection of social organization. Devotion to intellectual and esthetic values was a leisure-time affair, a badge of social distinction. Conversely, practical affairs, and particularly manual labor, were the proper business of slaves and peasants and commoners generally, who were either incapable of, or not destined for, a higher life.

This opposition between the life of leisure and the practical life carried with it momentous consequences, both for social matters and for education.

These consequences are symbolized, after a fashion, by the notion that the three R's are just "tool subjects." Perhaps one might say that in the domain of the practical life, insofar as this could be held apart from the higher life of culture, all education was just a tool for getting things done. For a long period it was not considered necessary that the common man should have any formal education at all. Later, as the social order became more complex, it was conceded that a knowledge of reading, writing, and arithmetic was a useful equipment. Beyond that all his knowledge, except what was handed to him on authority, was of a practical kind. He had a store of information about planting and reaping, about the treatment of colds, about how to get along with people, and the like. This kind of knowledge is sometimes called empirical and sometimes called pragmatic. It had a simple test. Knowledge is sound if things work out according to expectations. The common man, for example, could undertake to meet a person at sunrise, and he would consider his knowledge of sunrise valid or true if it served him in such ways. He would not be likely to consider that this knowledge depended on the question whether the sun "really" goes around the earth or *vice versa*.

For the leisure-class person the problem of knowledge and truth was less simple. To him the question of truth was not merely incidental to the business of getting the world's work done. Being separated from the world of practical affairs, he was compelled to contrive for his ideas some other meaning or function than usefulness in the control of experience. Moreover, as long as we make truth dependent on experience, we never get at anything absolute and final. To illustrate, the sun was first supposed to go around the earth; then, it was found that the earth goes around the sun; and no one can say how they will go after a group of relativists, like Einstein, have got in their work. Reliance on experience and practical requirements looked like a degradation of the sacred name of truth. It became necessary, therefore, to go in quest of "absolute" standards.

THE DOMINION OF ABSOLUTES

How this was done is exemplified in simple yet grand fashion by Plato's doctrine of Ideas. According to Plato, the everyday world in which we live is not itself reality, but a fleeting and distorted image or reflection of reality. The real world is supersensuous; it is non-material and unchangeable; it is made up of certain eternal and immutable essences, such as Truth, Goodness, and Beauty. These realities are called Ideas, for want of a better name. The name is perhaps intended to indicate their supersensuous and non-material character. These Ideas furnish us with standards. Our ideas of truth, goodness, and beauty are valid ideas, not by the test of experience but by the test of correspondence or conformity to these supreme essences which go by the same names.[1]

This doctrine of Ideas is of interest to us in the present connection, not because it gives us a better understanding of the world in which we live, but because it shows what happens when men turn their backs on everyday reality and try to lift themselves by their own bootstraps. The creation of this transcendental world was at the same time one of the most brilliant achievements and one of the major tragedies of human civilization. To what extent the intellectual capacity of the race was condemned to speculative sterility by the influence of this doctrine, no one can say. Since the aristocratic form of social organization prevailed practically everywhere during most of the past, some such course of development was perhaps inevitable. The particular form of

[1] Plato's *Dialogues: The Republic* (VII), *Meno, Phaedo.*

Plato's doctrine has long been a matter of merely historical interest, but its progeny was legion and is to be found everywhere. The whole tribe of "absolutes" in our Western world can probably claim kinship with these Platonic realities, from notions of absolute property rights to the absolutes of nationalistic or racial dictatorships and to the theological dictum that this vale of wrath and tears is a hopeless mess and heaven alone is our abiding city. Whatever the form, the common man is always told that his little affairs do not count in comparison with these august absolutes.

For a long time these absolutes had things pretty much their own way in the academic world. They had, indeed, frequent squabbles among themselves, but there was little disposition to challenge the principle of absolutism, in spite of the fact that no one has as yet succeeded in giving a convincing account of what an absolute is really like as a "real" thing. Plato was a poet in temperament as well as a philosopher and his access to the world of Ideas seems to have been through a kind of semi-mystical adoration. His successors were often more hard-headed, but they were not any more successful in making these absolutes meaningful; which is perhaps not surprising, since the attempt to get beyond experi-

ence seems bound to take us—in Hegelian phrase—
into a night where all cows are black.

The common man was, of course, too inarticulate,
and at the same time too much in awe of his betters,
to challenge the conclusions of the wise men. Since
he has been coming into his own, however, he has
become more sensitive to the conflict between the
aristocratic way of life and the way of life where,
as a practical man, he lives and moves and has his
being. This sensitiveness makes him more skeptical,
even if he cannot match theory with theory; and he
has lost his awe sufficiently to engage, on occasion,
in ridicule. This perhaps explains the paradoxical
attitude which was mentioned previously. Scholarship and culture are prized by him, yet its products
are stigmatized with such epithets as "highbrow"
and "ivory tower." A highbrow, so we have been
told, is a person who has been educated beyond the
limits of his intelligence. This is an irreverent way
of saying that scholarship and culture tend to become entangled with a mythological realm of trans-
experiential reality, which is too remote and too sub-
lime to be checked and tested by ordinary experience. When or insofar as this happens, higher education becomes a kind of cult in which human
values evaporate into a set of abstractions. Empha-

sis on scholarship or theory does not in itself make a person inept, because sound theory always keeps in touch with the relevant facts. But theory which loses this contact by going off in a different direction is deserving of distrust.

The present-day reaction of the common man may perhaps be construed as a hopeful sign that man will presently engage in a direct struggle with himself to keep from being subjugated and exploited by the figments of his own imagination. Nature has proved to be a less formidable enemy than the absolutes which have kept him in bondage from the time of Plato down to our present dictatorships. To use the vernacular, he has never dared to call his soul his own. At the behest of authority he has on occasion repudiated the evidence of science and experience, with all the assurance of the much-quoted rustic who ended his inspection of the giraffe by saying: "There ain't no such animal." The same blind obedience has caused him to believe that fire and slaughter and the degradation of human beings were in accordance with the will of an infinitely tender Providence. In matters of art he—or more frequently she—still struggles pathetically to like the things that have the right labels, even at the cost of those healthy reactions which once prompted

Justice O. W. Holmes to say, after he had seen a vaudeville show: "Thank God, I am a man of low tastes."

THE CHOICE REQUIRED

Progressive education is confronted with the choice of becoming the avowed exponent of democracy or else of becoming a set of ingenious devices for tempering the wind to the shorn lamb. If democracy is to have a deep and inclusive human meaning, it must have also a distinctive educational system.

Since the whole weight of tradition is on the side of absolutes, which are abstractions that served to maintain an aristocratic form of society, such a system must have direct and constant reference to the conflict between the aristocratic and the democratic ways of life. It must have a psychology based on the conception of knowledge and truth as functions in the control of experience—the kind of psychology which is pointed toward in what is sometimes called "organismic" psychology. It must have a theory of values which has as its center the continuous improvement of human living through voluntary reciprocity or the constant widening of common interests and common concerns. Lastly, it must undertake to point out how the acceptance of such a standard for growth and progress requires continuous and frequently extensive reconstruction or revision of traditional beliefs and attitudes, in accordance with growing insight and changing circumstances. In a word, progressive education must become clearly conscious of the implications contained in its basic attitude and to use these implications as a vantage point from which to reorganize its thinking and its procedures.

CHAPTER II

THE PARTING OF THE WAYS

DIVIDED LOYALTIES

In the preceding chapter it was pointed out that the rise of the common man has been a disturbing factor, in education as elsewhere. In some respects the effect of this disturbance is perhaps most evident on the level of higher education. The college of today is a very different institution from what it was in the past. The curriculum has not merely been enriched; it has been transformed in the direction of giving amazing recognition to utilitarian subjects. Courses ranging in content all the way from stable manure to multidimensional space may now be counted towards an A.B. degree. But in this array of offerings it is difficult to discern a controlling ideal. Practical and technical courses stand side by side with the older "humanities." The advantages of education have been demonstrated too

often to admit of serious doubt; but the layout of
courses suggests that our colleges are trying to serve
both the ideals of the past and the conflicting ideals
of the present.

This suspicion is justified. Our colleges are crea-
tures of divided loyalties, with no clear realization
that they are engaged in supporting two conflicting
and irreconcilable ways of life. On the one hand
are the demands of our traditional loyalty to the eternal verities. But on the other hand are the demands
made by this world of flux in which we actually
live. These demands are growing in number and
volume, and it is becoming increasingly difficult to
silence them by placing them in contemptuous contrast with the unchanging serenity of the beautiful
isle of somewhere. The situation is confusing because the basic issue is not brought out into the open.
The result is that the colleges no longer know what
they are for. They cling to the old and at the same
time cultivate an evangelistic or Rotarian spirit of
"service." The danger is, of course, that of falling
between two stools. The college neither has the effectiveness of a technical school nor succeeds any too
well in creating the intellectual atmosphere which
is supposed to differentiate the college from an ath-
letic union or a country club.

A RETURN TO PLATO?

This situation has called forth a proposal for remedy[1] which has attracted considerable attention. According to Dr. Hutchins, the chief trouble with higher education in this country is precisely that it has carried the spirit of accommodation too far. In trying to serve passing demands and imaginary needs it has lost sight of its true function. The college tries to be all things to all men because it has ceased to be anything in itself. It is in process of forgetting its real mission, which is the pursuit of truth. Translated into terms of our previous discussion, Dr. Hutchins' plea is for a return to the Platonic fourth-dimensional realities. Education must stop chasing rabbits and cultivate devotion to eternal and immutable truth. The appropriate concern of education is not with utilities or needs, but with the unchanging principles underlying the domains of nature, social relations, and the fine arts. This supersensuous world is held to be accessible through intellectual effort. By applying himself the student can come face to face with the true and the good and the beautiful as eternal and unchanging essences and thus become emancipated from the ob-

[1] R. M. Hutchins, *Higher Learning in America.*

sessions and distortions of time and circumstance. The central task of education, therefore, so Dr. Hutchins concludes, is with basic principles, which are valid at all times and in all places and for every manner and condition of men.

That this point of view is likely to have a certain appeal it would be useless to deny. Many educators have doubtless grown weary of the confusion which pervades present-day education. To those who demand certainty it offers the prospect of leaning on the Everlasting Arms. Perhaps all of us feel the pull of the intellectual habits and attitudes which link us with this age-old tradition. But there is also what has been called the moral obligation to be intelligent. What, as a matter of hard, sober sense, is meant by the claim that truth, goodness, and beauty are objective and eternal facts? What are these fundamental principles which are so often mentioned and never explained or illustrated? What assurance have we that this invitation to return to a mystic absorption in eternal verities is not a betrayal of democracy, by deflecting attention from the issues and the obstacles involved in the struggle for the more abundant life?

We may concede that Dr. Hutchins has rendered a service to higher education in challenging it to state its program. At present, as he contends, it is oscillating between the pursuit of truth and practicality. This dualism of ends, it may be observed, corresponds closely to the contrast between leisure occupations and the practical life which was maintained by the Greeks. The remedy, however, is not to eliminate practicality and thus to return to the intellectual ideals of Plato and Aristotle and St. Thomas Aquinas. An alternative is offered, if we will take the trouble to consider the implications of modern science, which has not only contributed enormously to the enrichment of the practical life, but has opened the way to the organization of the whole of life on a different basis from the past.

Working Concepts vs. Absolute Principles

One of the striking tendencies in the development of modern science is the tendency to shy away from the notion of absolute truth and to treat hypotheses or theories as merely "operational" concepts. When we say, for example, that the earth is round, this statement is not intended as a reference to a Platonic realm of unchanging essences, but simply as an assertion that the concept of roundness is a dependable guide for projected operations. On the basis of this concept we can circumnavigate the globe, calculate the length of day and night for any given point at any given time, and do various other things of an "operational" kind. Science, therefore, is, first of all, a refinement of the procedures of the practical man. But in its bearings or implications it is vastly more than that. Since it shuts the door on absolutes, it makes all truth subject to the same test. It brings truth, goodness, and beauty down from the clouds and sets the stage for a reinterpretation of them in terms of a better associated or democratic living.[2]

From this point of view, the vice of "practicality" is not that it has to do with practical things, but that it conceives its ends too narrowly. Thus the farmer who is interested only in making money is "practical" in an invidious sense. There is no reason, however, why he should not concern himself with farming as a whole way of life. In his study of the sciences that are basic to farming, he may have his attention directed to the "operational" character of scientific concepts; in the study of co-operative marketing, crop control, and what not, he may be made acquainted with the view that the test of moral goodness is related to the extension of voluntary

[2] John Dewey, *The Quest for Certainty* (V). J. W. Bridgeman, *The Logic of Modern Physics* (I, II).

co-operation and common interests among men; in connection with the esthetic side of farm life, he may be asked to consider whether art is anything more than certain devices for the enhancement of appreciations. The difference between a liberal and a technical education is not that the former devotes itself to the pursuit of truth, while the latter seeks practical results. Technical education becomes liberal to the degree that it leads the student to the realization that it involves a whole way of life.

The astonishing thing about Dr. Hutchins' proposal is that it ignores so completely the possibility of any alternative to his conception of truth. It is assumed that the rejection of this conception commits us to chaos and anti-intellectualism. There is scarcely a hint that the sciences are pointing to a theory of truth which is divorced from these ghostly absolutes of the past. It is understandable that a theory such as Plato's doctrine of Ideas should be evolved when the world was still young. It is less understandable that a modern man should pass by all that science and racial experience may have to say on the subject and lightheartedly assume that this ancient theory makes sense or that these absolutes are anything but human prejudices invested with a halo and put on ice. The whole drift of modern science is toward the conclusion that the point of reference in every investigation falls within our three-dimensional world; and that our tests and standards are not derived from elsewhere but are constructed as we go along.

At all events, this general tendency is in the field and is running strong, even though it is still largely inarticulate and unformulated. It maintains that man's future is in his own hands; that social and ethical and esthetic principles are neither handed to him ready-made nor so embedded in the structure of things that he need but look in order to discover them. He must create and recreate them for himself, in the course of racial history, out of the raw material of experience, just as, through the centuries, he has created, out of his cumulative experience, an industrial order and systems of money and credit. It is fair to assume that much of the indifference of college students to intellectual interests is due to the highbrow quality which these interests carry over from the past. They have a musty smell which is vaguely reminiscent of morgues and museums.

While the discussion, up to this point, has been conducted chiefly on the level of higher education, it is important to note that the issue involved is by no means confined to higher education but extends all the way down the educational ladder. The reason is simple. Life, after all, does not lend itself freely to such oppositions as that between the higher and the lower life. The practical man of former times was not shut in entirely to his practicality. Besides being a worker, he bore certain relationships to state and church. He was taught to respect property, to obey his feudal lord, to accept the deliverances of the church. The principles which he was expected to follow in these matters were not derived from his "practical" life, but were handed down to him by some authority. While these principles have changed in the course of the years, there is still a chasm between them and the democratic point of view discussed previously. Since education is supposed to prepare for membership in the social order, the issue raised by democracy is relevant all along the line. It is only too obvious that the reorganization called for by the principle of democracy has not yet been completed.

It goes without saying that the common man was not always disposed to accept the status which, as was sometimes alleged, the Lord had assigned to him. But since he was not a philosopher, and since modern science had not yet arrived to furnish him with helpful hints, the common man was in no position to challenge the doctrine of absolutes by which he was being victimized. He took refuge, therefore, in contriving a few absolutes of his own. As against the doctrine of the divine right of kings, he announced the doctrine of "consent by the governed" and the inalienable right to life, liberty, and the pursuit of happiness. From the laws of society he made appeal to the "law of nature." When suffering from religious oppression, he took his stand on "freedom of conscience." In other words, he found that two could play at this game. As slogans or war cries his absolutes often were tremendously useful. The practical difficulty about these new absolutes was that, if they succeeded in making themselves prevail, they became a source of new tyrannies and new obstacles, as is the way with all absolutes. In this country, for example, the right of contract, which is alleged to be an inalienable right and a precious possession of the common man, has frequently been interpreted so as to legalize injustices against him.[3]

Is Progressivism a New Absolutism?

As might be expected, this situation is reflected in education. The most notable example is that of Rousseau. In his revolt against the tyrannies and

[3] Dewey and Tufts, *Ethics*, pp. 503-507.

brutalities of the social order of his day, Rousseau made his appeal, not to the principle of democracy, but to the sacred and inviolable nature of the individual. Over against the absolutes of the social order he placed the alleged absolute of human nature. Education, in his view, must be conducted, not according to the behests of vested interests, which used the creed of absolutism to entrench themselves, but according to the nature of childhood. This latter meant, in effect, that the child should be permitted to grow up in his own way, without being subjected to "impositions" by others. Since man is created in the image of God, the best way to educate him is to permit this image to express itself according to its own inherent nature. All this obviously comes close to saying that we should not educate at all.

This point of view received reinforcement at a later time from the doctrine of instincts, which, however, provided a different set of blue-prints for "human nature." Instead of regarding the baby as an image of God, the instinct psychology viewed him as a bundle of instincts, which had a certain quality of finality. It was argued, for example, that war and the profit motive were ineradicable parts of the social order, because they were based, respectively, on the instinct of fighting and the instinct of acquisitiveness. The educational views of Rousseau and of the instinct psychologists were much the same, however, in that both claimed to find in the child the only clues to an educational program.

This is absolutism all over again. If we may trust the findings of modern psychology and the social sciences, it is just as impossible to find educational objectives by inspecting the individual child as it is by looking for them in a transcendental realm. The most that the study of childhood can reveal is the nature of the raw material with which we have to work. If we expect such study to produce an educational program, then, no matter how excellent our intentions may be, the interests of democracy are bound to suffer. A democratic program of education must necessarily rest on the perception that democracy is a challenge to all forms of absolutism, that it has its own standards, ideals, and values, and that these must pervade the entire program from end to end.

It is precisely at this point that progressive education is in the doldrums. The uncertainty here is the chief cause of the confusions and contradictions which make it so difficult to define the movement. The faith of progressive education in the individual, and in the power of intelligence to create new standards and ideals in terms of human values and in accordance with changing conditions, entitles it to consideration as expressive of the spirit of democracy. As against this, however, stands the fact that it has never completely emancipated itself from the individualism and absolutism of Rousseau. Instead of turning to the ideal of democracy for guidance, it has all too often turned to the individual. It has nurtured the pathetic hope that it could find out how to educate by relying on such notions as interests, needs, growth, and freedom. The futility of this is reflected in the excrescences that have grown up about the movement. But there are also unmistakable indications that the movement will be guided more directly and more consciously by a social ideal in the future than it has been in the past.

CLARIFYING THE UNDERLYING PHILOSOPHY

The time has come when progressive education must undertake, in the interests of its future development, to clarify its underlying philosophy. This philosophy centers on two basic propositions. One of these has to do with the nature of the learning process; the other relates to the social implications of the doctrine that the maximum development of the individual is the supreme aim or purpose of education.   Both of these propositions must be protected against the persistent tendency toward misinterpretation in terms of the individualism and absolutism which has become associated with the name of Rousseau.

With respect to the nature of learning, we have become familiar with the doctrine that learning is tied up in some way with doing.   As a protest against "passive" learning and uninspired reciting, the doctrine has significance and validity.   Unless it is made clear, however, in what way doing is related to learning, there is every likelihood that doing will be mistaken for learning and that the ends of education will thus once again meet with frustration.

In the interests of brevity we may assume without discussion that learning is not a matter of training hypothetical "faculties" nor yet of producing "conditioned reflexes" in order that the affairs of every-day living may be carried on with a minimum of attention and reflection.   Stated in positive terms, learning is a process by which experiences are changed so as to become more serviceable for future guidance. The baby that gets scratched by the cat, for example, acquires a transformed experience of the cat.   The first experience of the cat, as an object to be reached for and handled, is followed by an experience with a different set of reactions, by virtue of which the cat appears as an object that is "treacherous" or "hurtful" or "nasty." The cat *looks* different, and the "feeling-tone" of the experience is different. The experience has acquired a new meaning and a new value. All learning is a matter of making over experiences in terms of what we can do with things and situations or in terms of what they will do to us; and so this conception of learning links up directly with the doctrine of "operational concepts," which is a denial of all absolutes.

As applied to formal education, this view of learning explains and justifies the emphasis on "activity" programs and on the insistence that the activities of the school must be organized with primary reference to the purpose of maintaining or carrying on a certain way of life. The day-by-day experiences of the pupil must be made over in a certain way, through living and doing. This way of life, if progressive education is to remain true to its basic point of view, is the "democratic" way, as previously discussed. Thus the theory of learning and the theory of social organization implicit in progressive education become inseparably intertwined.

Practice, however, lags behind theory. Individualism has a tendency to be satisfied if pupils are engaged in happy and interesting activities. It tolerates an incredible amount of whim and bad manners because "maximum development" is tacitly assumed to be controlled from "within." In terms of its own theory of learning, progressive education is in duty bound to repudiate the whole contrast between "within" and "without" as a vicious metaphor. The appropriate distinction is between the experience of the learner as it actually occurs and the wider potential experiences for which the present experience is a stepping-stone and which stand for "maximum development" or "true selfhood." But it must not be overlooked that "maximum development" is in itself an empty phrase. It can easily be used as a justification for a program of disconnected activities or for a program of indoctrination in traditional attitudes and points of view.

Progressive education stands at the parting of the ways. The issue of democracy is becoming more insistent in all the relations of life. It implies a social and an educational philosophy which needs to be formulated and applied. If progressive education can succeed in translating its spirit into terms of democratic philosophy and procedure, the future of education in this country will be in its hands. On the other hand, if it persists in a one-sided absorption in the individual pupil, it will be circumnavigated and left behind. The purpose of the succeeding chapters will be, first, to show how the lack of an effective social ideal has led it into byways and blind alleys, and, secondly, to furnish at least a general indication of the direction which the movement must take if its present promise is to be fulfilled.

CHAPTER III

THE DOCTRINE OF INTEREST

Modern psychology has made us familiar with the notion that the living being is a center of energy which seeks expression through the medium of the environment in which it happens to be placed. Anyone who will take the trouble to watch the behavior of a small child for ten minutes will get ample illustration of what is meant. The observer will also get concrete examples of the absorption and concentration which we call interest and which is more easily illustrated than defined.

The normal result of such activity is some form of learning. Educators are generally agreed that learning is more effective if it is the expression or outcome of these drives or urges which are accountable for the phenomenon of interest. Our concern at the moment is with the fact that activity involving interest is conditioned by the *environment* as well as by the bodily constitution of the learner.

ENVIRONMENT CONDITIONING INTEREST

The implications of this proposition are far-reaching. What we call the environment of the average person is both physical and social. The social environment, as well as the physical, presents a wide range of variation and is enormously important in shaping the development of the individual. About the only off-hand generalization that we can make with respect to these various forms of social organization is that each embodies in some manner a specific way of life. This way of life has to do both with the means of making a living and with ideals, values, standards.

To the person born into a social environment and growing up in it the particular way of life going on about him normally becomes a matter of interest. There is no mystery about this, since the environment is to the growing child an opportunity to secure an outlet for the energies which crave expression. The youngster is full of energy, but these energies are for the most part unorganized and undirected. Hence our young hopeful is prepared, like St. Paul, to be all things to all men. He is capable of developing intense enthusiasms for the most diverse kinds of activities and ideals, because these

provide release of activity and thus take on interest
and value. If we add to this the commendation
which he is likely to receive for achievements that
conform to socially approved standards, it is easy to
see that the way of life to which he belongs is bound
to have an overpowering influence on him. The relation of activity to a way of life, therefore, is of
basic significance for the concept of interest and for
our understanding of the place or function of formal
education in the social order.

FORMER LIMITS OF SCHOOL RESPONSIBILITY

One inference that seems to be warranted by these
facts is that schools were originally mere adjuncts
to the way of life going on outside of the school,
and, in a sense, relatively unimportant adjuncts at
that. During the entire prehistoric period of human
existence education was in the main a matter of
direct participation in the life of the group. Schools
did not come in until the advance of civilization had
introduced certain special requirements, notably
those represented by the three R's, which could not
be conveniently met otherwise. In effect the chief
purpose of the school was to reinforce the way of
life that was practiced by the community by supply-

ing certain skills and information required by this way of life. While this was a more or less necessary function, the place of the school in the whole scheme of things was somewhere on the periphery and not at the center.

Perhaps it is permissible to introduce some personal recollections at this point. In the days of my early youth I once taught a rural school. As far as I know, it was fairly representative of the little red schoolhouse that we have heard so much about. My school wasn't red, but it was a one-room affair, it was rural, and it had a curriculum that was limited pretty much to the three R's. Teaching that school, as I look back on it now, was simplicity itself. I assigned the lessons and heard the recitations—that was my job. The pupils learned the assignments and did the reciting—that was their job. When that was over we knocked off and called it a day.

If my methods were simple, my job was likewise simple. There was a great deal of education going on in that community, but most of it had no relation to my school. The pupils learned a great deal about vocations, for example, but my school offered no courses in vocations. The young people learned about them at home—out in the fields and in the kitchen. They got a complete set of ideas about

economics and government, but they didn't get them
from me. They got them at home. It was the father's
prerogative to explain the tariff system and to
warn the boys against the Democrats. In matters
of religious beliefs the father was usually somewhat
less fluent and convincing, but he did what he could,
and the rest was looked after by church and Sunday
school. Manners and customs were taught and rig-
idly enforced by the community. In brief, all the
heavy work in education was done outside the
school. My task was simply to take care of certain
skills and information which could not be handled
very conveniently at home. Those were "the good
old days" in education. A person could teach then
without feeling that the burden of the universe was
resting on his shoulders.

MOTIVATION IN EDUCATION ON THE FARM

Now let us look at that situation for a moment as
professional educators. The education going on outside of my school was in certain fundamental respects a beautiful, albeit unconscious, exemplification
of Progressive doctrine. With respect to method, it
relied on the familiar principle of learning by doing,
and it practiced the doctrine that education is a form

of present living. The method, I may add, justified all the claims that have ever been made for it. It never occurred to me, for example, to teach respect for labor. That was amply taken care of without any help from me. I might as well have undertaken to teach ducks how to swim. Laziness was a deadly sin in that community. Habits of industry were, therefore, no problem, except when it came to reading, writing, and arithmetic. The young people learned things by having them bred into the bone.

With respect to the purpose or aim of education the situation was equally simple. The purpose of the process was to take children into full partnership in the life of the community. The aim, as we sometimes phrase it nowadays, was participation. In its purpose this education was both definite and effective.

The purpose of this discussion is not, of course, to indulge in a nostalgic lament for the good old days. This old-fashioned scheme of informal education, in spite of its effectiveness and definiteness, had certain serious defects. In some respects it was just another instance of the subordination of the individual to a pre-established scheme of things. Little attention was paid, for example, to individual differences, except that the bright boy was likely to be considered as possible material for a clergyman. There was no serious effort to provide scope for special aptitudes that might find expression within the framework of the existing agricultural life; such scope as is offered, for example, by scientific agriculture or home economics or the field of esthetics. In theology the door was closed and barred as tightly as possible against changes whose claims were based on new knowledge or new conditions. Nor was the work of the school so closely articulated with the life outside as to provide a carry-over of interest and purpose. Yet this reference to rural conditions is pertinent because it provides a different perspective on the question of interest.

How is motivation to be secured? We have filled heaven and earth with debates over the problem of interest. In the rural environment just referred to there was no such problem. Who ever heard of a farm being run on the basis of immediate interests? Milking the cows and feeding the pigs were not projects; they were just plain chores. They were done, not in response to "felt needs," but in conformity to a schedule. These chores were bound up with the whole way of life on the farm. This way of life was the natural and normal outlet for energy and ambition. The average boy on the farm, in his eagerness to be rated as a man, was willing to endure a great deal of strenuous work and monotonous drudgery in order to secure recognition. There was no conscious attempt to relate every phase of the work on the farm to interest, because the larger or more remote interest was expected to sustain the individual in the performance of disagreeable tasks.

In other words, the doctrine of interest may be interpreted in either of two ways. It may be construed to mean either that every activity must be motivated by immediate interest or that every activity must have a recognized bearing on a way of life which the individual accepts as his own. It is chiefly in the latter sense that the occupation of farming is related to interest. Immediate interests, of course, are not excluded and may have great significance. But they must either be derived from or be merged into the larger interest if there is to be a dependable basis for continuity of effort, without which there can be no adequate sense of responsibility and discipline of character.

Confusion in Modern Schools and Life

Now contrast this with the situation that is presented in a modern progressive school. The latter is an *artificial* situation, not in any invidious sense, but in the sense that it is a substitute for the life outside of the school. To provide such a substitute was an inescapable necessity. But the fact that it is a substitute introduces certain important differences. What is substituted is not some implied way of life, but a series of discrete activities. Hence there is not the same practical reason for doing things as there is outside the school. There is not the incentive that comes from direct participation in the activities of adults. There is, in short, no adequate continuity between the school and what may, by contrast, be called "real life." Yet incentives must be present in order to prevent school work from degenerating into meaningless routine. Consequently appeal has been made to immediate interests, which provided an escape from the difficulty but which could hardly be expected to go the whole way. To interpret the doctrine of interest as meaning that all activity must be motivated by immediate and spontaneous interests is to misrepresent it. There is no warrant for such interpretation in the facts of everyday life. We have this doctrine of interest because we have "progressive" schools.

The chasm between the school and the world has been widened by the changes that have taken place in modern life. Our population has become urbanized and industrialized. Our young people are deprived of constant and intimate association with adults in common pursuits. The lives of parents and children have, of necessity, grown apart. Except for Sundays and holidays the children of many families hardly know what the head of the family looks like by daylight. In addition to this our young people are exposed to all kinds of conflicting opinions and practices, on the streets, on the playgrounds, and in the marketplace. The old unity of life has been largely lost.

This is the situation confronting our schools. Since their concern is, in some way or other, with the "development of the individual," we might reasonably expect the school to help the pupil to gain for himself, in improved form, the unity without which life can have neither dignity nor seriousness of purpose. Unfortunately the popular conception of interest becomes a formidable obstacle.

Materials for study are, indeed, freely drawn from everyday affairs. But the idea of a controlling way of life fades out and reliance is placed instead on immediate interests. The result is that "interest" is transformed into a mystical driving force which needs only to be released in order to produce automatically fruits worthy of education. The pupils must plan everything themselves; they must not be held responsible for the performance of their tasks; they must be permitted to reduce the teacher's function to continuous improvisation.

The end-product of all this obviously cannot be, except by accident, anything that even remotely resembles a way of life. It is bound to be lacking in seriousness and continuity of purpose and a sense of responsibility. All this is alleged to be required by progressive education and is defended in the name of "respect for personality." The pupil apparently is not credited with sufficient seriousness of purpose or capacity for responsibility to make his personality worthy of respect. It is perhaps fortunate that the pupil usually does not know when he is being insulted.

True and False Guidance of Interest

This criticism is not directed against the doctrine of interest but against its misinterpretation. The only sure basis for the guidance of interest is to be found in the relation between interest and the need of developing or regaining a unified way of life. Interests normally need reinforcement through a constantly widening perception of their meanings or implications. Such widening of insight is not a

merely quantitative affair; it calls for the reorganization or reinterpretation of other beliefs and attitudes
which get in the way.

The nurture of artistic interests, for example, is
hampered by economic standards of success. Our
patriotism is weakened by sentiments of interna-
tionalism. Our religious beliefs are toned down by
the naturalistic attitude which has become associated
with the name of science. Our enthusiasm for the
social control of industry and for social security is
dampened by the tradition of individualism in business. Every concern of life needs normally to be
adjusted to other concerns; this requires painstaking and sometimes disagreeable reinterpretation of
values, but leads eventually to what we have called
a whole way of life. Otherwise these various concerns get into one another's way, and we then have
the paradox that, with all our emphasis on interest,
the outcome is not a release of energy but a kind of
mental paralysis. The trouble is, of course, that instead of having a unified pattern we have a welter
of patterns, which tend to neutralize one another.
The moral is that progressive education gets off the
track whenever it fails to keep alive a realizing sense
that it represents a distinctive and challenging way
of life.

Until within recent years progressive education has been conspicuously indifferent to the confusion in our cultural "patterns"; it has been individualistic and insensitive to the need of social reform. It has taken the framework of the present social system too much for granted. It has dealt so long with the child in abstraction from the confusions in our social *milieu* that it has become the victim of its habits. It has permitted so much sentimentality to grow up around the notion of the child that the term "child" is almost spoiled for sensitive people. And the irony of it all is that, in this one-sided devotion to the child, it has betrayed the child and deprived him of his birthright. He grows up in society, but he does not really belong to it. He finds himself in a civilization that is being rocked to its foundations, without knowing what he is for or what he is against. He goes into life without an encompassing faith, without objects of allegiance by which to shape his conduct.

It may be of interest to refer briefly, by way of contrast, to reports that come to us from other countries. In China, a few years ago, the students, at a time of crisis, laid themselves on the railroad tracks to keep trains from moving. The youth of Russia, so we are told, are aflame to maintain and promote communism against the wicked designs of capitalism. In Germany Naziism seems to have become a youth movement. One young German boy, according to a recent report, offered a prayer that he might die some time with a French bullet in his heart.

What do such things mean to us as educators? We have been sensitive to the importance of interest, but we have been singularly blind to the real character of interest. We have made no serious effort to provide young people with a gospel to live by. It is no accident that progressive education has made no conspicuous achievements on the level of adolescent youth. We have prided ourselves in the past on being "child-centered," on dealing with "the whole child," when, as a matter of fact, we have persistently slighted the kind of wholeness which is necessary in order to live intelligently and effectively in our present complex social order.

It would hardly be an exaggeration to say that the purpose of sound education is precisely to emancipate the pupil from dependence on immediate interests. A person cannot remain a baby all his life. He must learn to consider the bearings or consequences of what he does and to assume responsibility accordingly. This is the kind of thing that we mean when we speak of character and self-discipline—and of freedom, too. In cases of deliberate refusal to consider consequences which come within the range of his insight, he must be held to account. This is not imposition as long as we are dealing with consequences which, if given reasonable consideration by the pupil himself, would be of concern to him. In other words, the doctrine of interest is not to be construed as a justification for prolonging the period of infancy as much as possible. The basic concern of this doctrine is rather to make education a process centering on the continuous reconstruction of experience in the direction of a total pattern which derives its warrant, not from externally imposed authority, but from the exercise of the pupil's own intelligence.

An American Cultural Pattern

Obviously there is no room for such a doctrine of interest in a totalitarian state, in which the educational patterns are prescribed by a central authority. In this country we have no official creed to which everyone is expected to submit. What we have, on the contrary, is a tradition of democracy, which, despite all that has happened, is deeply embedded in the life of the American people. This tradition, though heavily overlaid with hangovers from the past, provides a far more generous scope for the exercise of individual intelligence. Freedom of speech and freedom of conscience have always been central tenets in our democracy. In practice, however, every freedom is subject to some kind of limitation, and a guiding principle is clearly necessary. What, then, is democracy?

Perhaps the best way to find an answer to this question is to consider the nature of an educational system which centers on the cultivation of intelligence, rather than submission to authority. Such a system recognizes no absolute or final truths, since these always represent authority in one form or another, and since they impose arbitrary limits on social progress and the continuous enrichment of experience. When interests or values collide, as they constantly do, and adjustments have to be made, social relations ordinarily enter in. The appropriate test for a good adjustment is not whether some sacrosanct value has been preserved unchanged, but whether progress has been made with respect to relations of reciprocity or co-operation with others for common ends. Our educational theory thus inevitably becomes a theory of social relationships, or a theory of democracy. Democracy as a tradition encourages reliance on intelligence in matters of education; and education, in turn, becomes an instrumentality for bringing democracy to a clear consciousness of its meaning and purpose.

This is the general direction in which progressive education must move if it is to remain faithful to its basic principles and ideals. The alternative is to keep forever rotating on the axis of "pupil interest." Progressive education has a unique opportunity of serving as a clearing house for the meaning of democracy and thus making a significant contribution toward bringing to fruition the great hope and promise of our American civilization.

CHAPTER IV

THE CONCEPT OF NEEDS

DESIRES OR NEEDS?

Any discussion among "progressive" educators is likely to bring in an early reference to the "needs" of pupils. In former years the term "felt needs" had considerable currency. The qualifying adjective had the great merit of providing an indication of what was meant by needs. A felt need was identical with desire; it was generated by the nature of the pupil and it pointed to an appropriate course of action. Since the desires are felt, we have a test for locating them; and since they are called needs we have the implication that we are dealing with a legitimate claim and that something should be done about it.

With this as a starting point, we need only bring in an absolute or two in order to settle the whole question of education out of hand. Rousseau found such an absolute in the doctrine that man is created in the image of God. This being so, the inference was reasonable that desires are the expression of this inherent pattern or divine image and therefore not subject to regulation of any kind. Education then becomes a process of providing these desires with an opportunity to grow and develop. Later, when the instinct theory came along, this simple theory of education remained essentially the same, since the instinct theory merely changed Rousseau's terminology without changing anything else. Human nature has the last word. Desires cannot be questioned. We can then identify education with the nurture of these "needs" or desires, in the comforting assurance that such identification has the endorsement both of the Almighty and of science.

In practice, however, the matter is not quite so simple. Granted that a felt need is a desire; are we really prepared to say that all desires are needs? The hankering of an old soak for another drink, for example, or the yearning of a small boy to punch his playmate's nose would hardly qualify as a real need in the mind of a pious educator. Even if we grant that those desires of which we disapprove are due to wrong influences in the environment and are not the product of the individual's real or "true" nature, we are still not out of the woods. To discriminate between good and bad desires means that we have some kind of standard which we did not get from a psychological inspection of desires but which was unobtrusively imported from somewhere else. This looks suspicious.

The situation gets still worse if we look into it further. Even if the desires which we encounter are innocent in themselves, their number and variety are such that we cannot give recognition to all of them. There are no discoverable limits to human desires. As William James says, "Not that I would not, if I could, be both handsome and fat and well dressed, and a great athlete, and make a million a year, be a wit, a *bon-vivant*, and a lady-killer, as well as a philosopher; a philanthropist, statesman, warrior, and African explorer, as well as a 'tone-poet' and saint. But the thing is simply impossible. The millionaire's work would run counter to the saint's; the *bon-vivant* and the philanthropist would trip each other up; the philosopher and the lady-killer could not well keep house in the same tenement of clay." [1]

In principle there is no difference in this respect between adults and younger people. When desires conflict, as they constantly do, a decision, to be intelligent, must be based, not on the quality or urgency of the desires, but on a long-range program. It is

[1] James, W., *Psychology*, Vol. I, p. 311.

the program, the more remote aim or purpose, that decides which desires are relevant and which are interlopers. Even so elementary a craving as hunger, for example, must be dealt with in this way. Perhaps the person concerned has what he considers to be an unesthetic tendency towards overweight; perhaps he deems it his duty to tighten his belt and help conserve the national food supply; perhaps he believes that eternal salvation can be won only through complete subjugation of the body; or again he may have a primitive conviction that the world owes him a living and act accordingly. It all depends. The fact that he is hungry does not in itself give a clue to his needs. The need is determined in each case by the end to be achieved, by the underlying philosophy. It is related that a man once said to the celebrated Dr. Samuel Johnson: "But, doctor, a man has to live!" To which the crusty old doctor replied: "Sir, I do not see the necessity."

By this time the doctrine of needs has become alarmingly complicated; but we have not yet reached the end of our troubles. It appears that, while we still talk about needs as clues to educational objectives, we are not only less inclined than formerly to take the "feltness" of a desire as evidence of a need, but recognize that a need may be a real need without being felt at all. Thus a man may be deemed to be greatly in need of a noble woman who loves him and has faith in him, even though the man himself be wholly unable to diagnose his case in any such fashion. Guidance work often has to do with the discovery of needs which are not recognized as such by the persons concerned. Some standard is necessary for discriminating between real and fictitious needs, just as a standard was previously found necessary for distinguishing between good and bad desires, or between desires which should receive preferential treatment and those which should not. Instead of finding in felt desire the answer to the pedagog's prayer, we have merely made two—or even three—problems grow where one grew before.

The moral is that the only way to discover a need is in terms of a "pattern" or scheme of values or an inclusive philosophy of some kind.

Let us suppose, for illustration, that a youngster is found to be maladjusted with respect to parental relationships. What light does this shed on his "needs"? This depends altogether on our theory of what these relationships ought to be. According to one view, he may be sadly lacking in the virtue of obedience to parental authority. According to another view, he may be in urgent need of a clearer insight into the limitations of this authority, so that he may persist in his course without being oppressed by a sense of guilt. Either of these views will provide a basis for the determination of needs, but neither one can be regarded as inherent in the nature of the individual or in the cosmic structure of the universe.

FISHING IN THE WRONG POOL

Studies of adolescence may be immensely valuable as portrayals of the difficulties that beset modern youth. But it is misleading to call them studies of needs, because the needs still remain to be determined after the investigation is completed. The claim that needs are discoverable in this way would have to be rated, not as a scientific truth, but as academic bootlegging. To expect "needs" to emerge from such studies is like expecting an architectural design to result from a study of the structural materials that are to be used for a building.

Nevertheless the notion that educational needs can be determined by studying the individual still persists. The present-day educator, however, is generally less naïve than Rousseau or the instinct psychologists. He does not believe that there are patterns etched on the bosom of the individual, so to speak, and discernible to a trained and sympathetic eye. Nor does he assume that appropriate patterns are waiting in the environment to be picked up. His procedure is more complex. He seems to think that while neither the environment nor the individual, each in isolation, can provide a pattern, the pattern will somehow emerge if we study the two together; not by a process of interpretation, but by a process of discovery. In other words, the data can be depended on to dictate an educational program. This is "child-centeredness," in the objectionable sense, all over again. It is not a surrender of the old point of view, but a refinement of it.

It is high time to realize that examining a youngster to ascertain his needs is different from examining him, say, for adenoids. Shall we say, for example, that a pupil with a pronounced talent for business needs a commercial course, plus, perhaps, a sympathetic acquaintance with our tradition of rugged individualism, or a comprehension of the evils inherent in a system of free competition, or a realizing sense that the love of money is the root of all evil? The answer will not be revealed by any educational microscope. Yet something like this seems to be assumed whenever curriculum making is centered so largely on intensive studies of pupil needs. There is reason to fear that the greatest danger to the progressive movement at the present time is within its own household. Social extremity is the educator's opportunity; but this opportunity will fade away if the demand for a more adequate educational philosophy is deflected toward a renewed emphasis on pupil needs.

The True Concern of Education

We may grant, of course, that in specific situations, where the end in view may be taken for granted, it is entirely appropriate to speak of needs, since the end or purpose furnishes a point of reference for judging the needs. But to undertake to build an educational program by starting with needs is quite another matter. Unless we assume that there is a predestined end for human living and that we are in the know as to what this end is, there is no justification whatsoever for talking so blithely about needs. An authoritarian scheme of education could make excellent use of a doctrine of needs, for it would be in a position to know at every point what it was talking about. In a democratic system of education the situation is entirely different. We cannot start with needs, because needs must be determined with reference to the way of life which the pupil eventually adopts as his own and the choice that he will make cannot be presupposed from the outset. Instead of using needs as a starting point, we educate people in order that they may discover their needs.

The point at issue is far more than the verbal question of how the term "need" is to employed. It concerns the question of what education should be primarily concerned to achieve. The failure to emancipate ourselves completely from Rousseauism and the instinct psychology is responsible for most, if not all, of the weaknesses of the progressive movement in education. The attitude of superstitious reverence for childhood is still with us. The insistence that we must stick uncompromisingly at all times to the "needs" of childhood has bred a spirit of anti-intellectualism, which is reflected in the reliance on improvising instead of long-range organization, in the overemphasis of the here and now, in the indiscriminate tirades against "subjects," in the absurdities of pupil-planning, and in the lack of continuity in the educational program. It has frequently resulted in an unhealthy attitude towards children, an attitude which suggests that there is no such thing as a normal child, and that we must be everlastingly exploring his insides, like a Calvinist taking himself apart day after day to discover evidences of sin.

It is a commonplace that the infant's only chance to grow into a human being is through social relationships. This is only another way of saying that growth is not directed from within but by the "patterns" embodied in the social order. If we believe in progress in a democratic sense, we must believe that these patterns require continuous revision. As they actually exist in our complex modern world, they not only present conflicting types, but the basic patterns are severally incoherent and internally contradictory. In business, for example, we accept both the profit motive and the ideal of social service; in government we hold to both rugged individualism and the ideal of social security; in the field of esthetics we find that standards are both absolute and relative. Back of all this confusion lies the issue of democracy versus tradition, which must be the central concern of a democratic school.

In a properly organized program this issue will be the constant point of reference, instead of being merely appended, like the tail to the kite, as an additional "need" along with all the others. If we take democracy seriously, an understanding of this issue must be made our basic need, in terms of which all other needs are determined. Otherwise the concept of needs becomes a red herring drawn across the trail. What we need is a moratorium on needs, so that we can get down to serious business and develop the implications that are contained in the philosophy of progressive education.

CHAPTER V

EDUCATION AS GROWTH

Perhaps no trait or aspect of the progressive movement in education is more familiar or more characteristic than the doctrine that education is growth. This doctrine has served both as a declaration of war and as a declaration of faith. In its militant aspect, it has meant a repudiation of the notion that the purpose of education is to perpetuate the cultural patterns which happen to prevail in a given community. As a cult it has meant that education must be "child-centered," in the sense that our clues for educational procedures must be got from pupil interests and pupil needs. The advantage claimed for such an approach is that education becomes transformed from a formal drill into a process of actual living. It is controlled by no dominating or inclusive purpose other than his continuous growth. Hence the test for growth becomes more growth. Education is for the sake of further education.

All this is too familiar to require elaboration. Moreover, it embodies an important truth. The rejection of mechanistic conceptions which is implied in this emphasis on growth is finding strong support in the recent trend of development in the natural sciences and in psychology. This trend is clearly towards the notion of "adaptiveness" and "creativeness." In the field of social relations, the current tendency towards dictatorships is a further warning against the danger of hampering free growth by the imposition of ironclad prescriptions in matters of belief and conduct. The moral for education, so it is insisted, is that our first obligation is to protect the sacred principle of growth. ✓ The impetus in learning must come from the "inside" and not from the "outside"; that is, it must spring from a felt need for a new adjustment. The successive adjustments must be guided not by an antecedent teacher-imposed vision of some far-off divine event, but by the experienced exigencies of the successive situations as they arise.

To accept all this, however, does not settle the question of how the concept of growth is to function as a guiding principle in education. As a matter of fact, there is ground for the suspicion that it is frequently misused and thus may become on occasion an obstacle rather than a help. A review of the situation, therefore, requires a critical attitude toward the leaders and spokesmen of the progressive movement. But this cannot be helped if we are to get anywhere. As a teacher of pugilism said to an aspiring pupil: "Keep milling away; don't stop to pick out your friends."

What Is Growth?

In one of its aspects every new gospel is a protest against some current evil. In the present case the evil that is attacked is "imposition," and a contrast is set up between molding from without and self-determining growth from within. A teacher who takes it upon himself to make the pupil conform to some preconceived pattern commits a sin against the law of "growth." In such a case, "growth is regarded as *having* an end, instead of *being* an end. . . . Since growth is the characteristic of life, education is all one with growing; it has no end beyond itself. The criterion of the value of school education is the extent to which it creates a desire for continued growth and supplies means for making the desire effective in fact."[1] "The old teacher

[1] John Dewey, *Democracy and Education* (The Macmillan Co.), pp. 60, 62.

had no fear of imposing his ideas; that was what he was there to do. The newer teacher is trying always to build up a process more adequately creative and self-directing from within." [2] "According to the old philosophy, loyalties and truths were handed down to the people by leaders in authority. According to the new, the people adopt whatever allegiances and accept whatever truths they discover for themselves." [3]

This protest against "dictation" or "regimentation," however, is not the whole story. If we make the mistake of regarding it as such, we get the curious conclusion that teachers must do no teaching at all, since all teaching is an attempt to provide "external" guidance. All we can do, then, is to take our stand with Rousseau and leave things to "nature." But, as Dewey says: "Merely to leave everything to nature was, after all, but to negate the very idea of education; it was to trust to the accidents of circumstance." [4] Similarly, Kilpatrick affirms that "It is not necessary to argue that proper adult oversight with frequent active guidance is essential to

[2] W. H. Kilpatrick, *Remaking the Curriculum* (Newson & Co.), p. 55.

[3] Harold Rugg, *American Life and the School Curriculum* (Ginn & Co.), p. 271.

[4] Dewey, *op. cit.*, p. 108.

the achieving of well-integrated personalities in any family or school." [5]   And Rugg contends, still more sweepingly: "The education set up must be one that will perpetuate the democratic culture." [6]

In brief, when the topic of guidance is under consideration the emphasis shifts to a different point. "Growth" must be protected, not against interference from without, but against the wrong kind of interference, as, for example, the kind that substitutes rote learning for insight, or verbalization for thinking. But it is necessary to go further and protect growth against wrong thinking. No one would seriously contend that non-progressive schools do not go beyond the point of producing parrots or phonograph records. The progressive movement has no monopoly of thinking. Growth must be protected against vicious indoctrination, against thinking that is turned in the wrong direction, or against improper obstacles to the exercise of thinking. To secure the right kind of growth, the enlightened teacher apparently need not fear to "impose," but he must be careful, in Kilpatrick's phrase, not to "impose hurtfully." [7]   The contrast now is not a contrast between

[5] Kilpatrick, *op. cit.*, p. 74.
[6] Rugg, *op. cit.*, p. 265.
[7] Kilpatrick, *op. cit.*, p. 55.

the "external" and the "internal," but between a type of guidance of which we approve and a type of which we do not approve.

The term "growth," then, may mean either that the initiative comes wholly from the pupil or that the pupil responds satisfactorily to suggestions emanating from the teacher. As a consequence of this ambiguity teachers of the progressive persuasion are exposed to two evils. One is a superstitious reverence for "inner growth" which makes them encourage ignorant guessing and tedious fumbling on the part of pupils, when the situation calls for guidance. Another is a disposition to regard the pupils' ability to understand and accept the teacher's personal opinons and prejudices as evidence of "inner growth" under "wise guidance," and not as the thing that it really is.

Self-Direction vs. Guidance

On account of this confusion, the doctrine of growth, in its present form, becomes a positive obstacle to clear thinking on the part of the teacher. It prevents him from discovering that he needs a guiding social philosophy. If he is called upon to state what it is that wise guidance should seek to accomplish, he points to "inner growth" or "self-directing from within." But if it is argued that inner growth may take a variety of forms, he has recourse to "wise guidance." The fact that this is a process of drawing water from an empty well is obscured by a flow of criticism directed against "imposition," which sometimes means "telling" as over against problem-solving and discovery by pupil, and sometimes means wrong guidance. The strategy of such a procedure is analogous to that which, according to our logic text-books, was recommended by a lawyer to his colleague when he slipped him a note which read: "No case; abuse the plaintiff's attorney."

It is encouraging to note that the problem of direction seems to be receiving increasing attention in progressive circles. Kilpatrick's recent book, *Remaking the Curriculum,* however, does not, despite its numerous excellences, get beyond the familiar oscillation from inner growth to wise guidance and back again. Rugg likewise, to whom belongs the credit of having stressed the need of direction for a long time, recurs to the topic in his latest publication,[8] but apparently without scoring any marked advance.

[8] Rugg, *op. cit.*

RIDING TWO HORSES

As Rugg clearly perceives, education must be based on a social philosophy. Hence he insists that the schools must produce "Believers in the Democratic Vista." In discussing the content of this Vista, however, he takes his cue, not from the perennial struggle against absolutes, but from the empty concept of growth. A democratic social order, we are told, is made up of "Multitudes of Individuals"; which means that we are supposed to have a democracy if everyone grows or develops in accordance with an inner propulsion. What is asserted, in short, is that we must have a democracy but that it must not go beyond the teachings of Rousseau.

This naturally gets us into trouble at once. The teacher is charged with the twofold obligation of developing "Believers in the Democratic Vista" and of paying scrupulous respect to "self-direction from within." If, for example, a pupil should start to grow after, say, the pattern of Hitler, the teacher's loyalty to his task of producing believers in the democratic vista would require him to pull this pupil back firmly and start him off in the right direction. But his loyalty to the ideal of a social order made up of multitudes of individuals would require that the pupil be let alone. Apparently it is impossible to teach democracy without ceasing to be democratic. So where do we go from here?

As a suggestion from the sidelines, the comment might be offered that a more adequate definition of democracy would avoid this impasse. To exhibit the issue which is raised when democracy is viewed as a challenge to absolute standards is in itself no more a matter of imposition or indoctrination than the discussion of any other issue. We take too much upon ourselves if we announce that our purpose is to win "believers in the democratic vista." The teacher's work is done when he has made the issue clear as best he can. Education becomes propaganda when we set out deliberately to make converts; and, moreover, we get hopelessly messed up if the doctrine for which we seek converts is a doctrine that it is wrong to seek converts.

The moral is that oil and water won't mix. We cannot have growth that is directed entirely from within and also growth that is directed from the outside. The person who believes in growth entirely from within will be, as Rugg says, "a believer in the validity and value of every thought-out personal philosophy. He will admire the honesty and the beauty, the authentic inner truth, that emanate from another personality." [9]   This is just an elaborate way of saying that for such a person one truth is as good as another, since there is no test for truth save the detached individual himself.   If we start with a detached, metaphysical Self, as our heritage from Rousseau, this conclusion regarding truth is presumably logical.   It means, however, that the plea for the Democratic Vista becomes an argument for the proposition that it is important to believe in the unimportance of beliefs.   The Democratic Vista is introduced to provide proper direction for growth; and more specifically to protect the American people against dictatorships.   Guidance is needed; and so we move from growth to guidance.   But when we inquire into the nature of the guidance, we are referred back to growth.   In other words, democracy is advocated on the ground that social direction is needed in order to secure completely developed individuals; but the kind of development that is desired precludes the possibility of providing social direction.

This is a disappointing and unromantic ending for what promised to be a great crusade for democracy.   At the outset democracy is advocated on the

[9] Rugg, *op. cit.*, p. 279.

assumption that it embodies a great and universal truth; but presently it appears that each person has his own "truth," which is only a roundabout way of saying that it would be more sensible not to talk about truth or validity at all. Matters of this kind become as personal as preferences in neckties or underwear, and there is no reason whatever for getting "steamed up" about truth. The ambiguity in the notion of growth is apparent. When dictatorships are to be disposed of, then it becomes of the utmost importance to select the right or "true" pattern for growth. But when educational aims are under consideration, growth is its own end, with the disquieting implication that one pattern is as good as another.

GROWTH WHITHER?

It is high time to try to escape from the vicious circle which has resulted from the application of the notion of growth to education. If we take to heart Heine's prayer to be delivered from the Evil One and from metaphor, we may even find it advisable to abstain from the use of the term altogether—at least for a time. At any rate, progressive education may reasonably be expected, after a career of some thirty years, to have something more than the metaphor of growth to go by. We cannot keep perpetually rotating on the axis of "self-direction."

Where should the teacher try to steer this process of self-direction? That the teacher should aim at "wise influencing," at "better self-directing," and at "somewhat better lines" for self-direction would be disputed by nobody. But if the pupil is not guided by an inner light, we can scarcely assume that the teacher is so guided. As a matter of fact, the teacher is in pretty much the same fix as the pupil, unless we assume that participation in the progressive movement automatically provides a lamp for his feet.

The fact that the progressive movement has never come across with an adequate philosophy of education warrants the presumption that it does not have any. Moreover, the lack of a "felt need" in this respect leaves room for the suspicion that so far the real problem in guidance has been the problem of imposing the teacher's views on the pupil without getting caught in the act.

The concept of growth undoubtedly has its uses. The view that education is a process in which experience is being continuously reorganized presents a refreshing contrast to mechanical types of learning. This use of the concept, however, becomes abuse if we assume that growth, in some mysterious way, provides for its own direction. Profitable growth in our own day and age is growth toward a plan for living intelligently in a topsy-turvy world; and such growth must have reference to the issue of democracy, which, in one form or another, is cropping up everywhere and which is, by all odds, the most important issue confronting us at the present time.

CHAPTER VI

"TEACH THE CHILD, NOT THE SUBJECT"

To the casual observer, American education is a confusing and not altogether edifying spectacle. It is productive of endless fads and panaceas; it is pretentiously scientific and at the same time pathetically conventional; it is scornful of the past, yet painfully inarticulate when it speaks of the future. The tremendous activity now going on in education is evidence of far-reaching social changes, but we do not seem to know what these changes signify or how they are to be directed.

Two Modern Schools of Thought

In this welter of divergent and conflicting practices it is possible to discern two main tendencies or attitudes. One emphasizes the need of making education a direct preparation for life; the other emphasizes the importance of full and free development. The former prides itself on its application of scientific method to the problem of the curriculum; the latter poses as the champion of childhood's right to live a life of its own. Both make their appeal to psychology; and psychology, in a spirit of amiability born of mental confusion, gives its sanction and its blessing to them both. The psychology of habit formation justifies prescription and rigidity of procedure; the psychology of play and of adolescence gives warrant to freedom and the cultivation of initiative. Like the oracles of old, psychology requires its supplicants to assume personal responsibility for the interpretation of its cryptic principles. Both of these tendencies claim to be enlightened and progressive because of the conviction which they hold in common that traditional education is inadequate for present-day needs.

From one of these tendencies or movements comes the complaint that such ideals as "culture," "character formation," or even "utility" are too vague to be of use without detailed and painstaking analysis. These time-honored objectives of education must be resolved into a set of specifics, for the guidance of conduct in connection with the concrete situations which are encountered during the course of the day. The solution of educational problems, it is contended, lies in the application of scientific analysis. This view is known as the doctrine of specific objectives.

The other movement is progressive education, which joins in the attack on traditionalism, but for a different reason. It insists that traditional education disregards the nature of childhood by forcing it into a kind of straitjacket. Lessons are assigned as so much material to be learned, without reference to the laws or principles of mental growth. The whole process is mechanized, at the sacrifice of spirit or attitude, which is both a precious by-product and the chief abiding value of true education. The typical pedagog's concern over specific and tangible results betokens a lack of imagination and understanding. Real education has a spirit of its own, and God fulfils Himself in many ways.

THE BUGBEAR OF SUBJECT MATTER

According to both of these newer attitudes or movements in education, the fault with traditionalism is that it has been too much preoccupied with the subject that is taught. In the past it has been customary, in many subjects, to present the material to be studied as though the purpose in teaching it were to train specialists. To the specialist in chemistry, for example, the law of atomic weights is a fact of peculiar importance, since it can be used as an instrument for further research in the field of chemïstry. Since research is the specialist's business, he organizes his knowledge of the subject in such a way as to make it an efficient tool for his purposes, and his way of organizing knowledge is what we call scientific organization. In brief, the specialist seeks to organize his subject matter so that he can make deductions from it, for purposes of explanation and prediction, since this is a great help in research. To teach with the emphasis on this kind of organization is presumably an instance of what is meant by teaching the subject instead of teaching the child.

It appears, however, that the average pupil does not approach the subject with the mental set of the specialist, and so this organization is likely to be unsuited to him. Consequently, the doctrine of specific objectives holds that the organization should be determined by "functional" needs—the needs of the farmer, the apothecary, the house keeper. This view is held to be defensible on two grounds: (a) it is practical, and (b) the applicability of such knowledge is more likely to arouse the respect and the interest of the pupil.

The competing progressive doctrine, however, maintains that the central consideration is still subject matter whether it is selected with reference to "logical organization" or with reference to "adult needs." The only way to escape from the tyranny of subject matter, so it is insisted, is to select with reference to the needs and interests of the pupil immediately concerned, and not with reference to the needs of adult life. It is only when we do this that we really teach, for then we teach the child instead of teaching the subject.

WHAT OF SCIENTIFIC ORGANIZATION?

There is reason to think that this assault on "scientific organization" has gone much too far. Nevertheless, the revolt against traditionalism in education is too widespread and too persistent to be dismissed as due to the vagaries of modern pedagogy. In fact, the dissatisfaction seems to be gathering strength. During recent years even the sacred precincts of the college have been invaded with the demand that college teaching be "vitalized" and brought into close relation to "life." It is quite likely that the critics of the college have no clear idea of what they want, but the fact that they want it and want it so insistently is of significance. It is just another indication that our educational system has something the matter with it. Education, it seems, has not kept pace with the social changes that are going on. If we are to judge intelligently of educational reforms, we must take account of these changes. As Lincoln said in the opening sentence of his famous "House Divided" speech: "If we could first know where we are and whither we are tending, we could better judge what to do and how to do it."

To know where we are and whither we are tending would undoubtedly require extraordinary sagacity. There are, however, certain high spots in the present situation that invite reflection.

To begin with, the popular demand for education is clearly not a spontaneous outburst of enthusiasm for abstract scholarship. If we ascribe it to the realization that present economic conditions place a premium on extensive educational training, we seem forced to the conclusion that training on the basis of specific objectives would impose a serious handicap on the pupil.

The ideal of vocational efficiency has undergone considerable transformation during recent years. The test is nothing so simple as the ability to step into a job. Representatives of industry are beginning to warn us that narrow training defeats its own purpose. Conditions in industry are changing so rapidly that the problem of enabling the individual to readjust himself as circumstances may require becomes a matter of primary importance. The demand is for "free intelligence" rather than for skills in connection with established patterns.

This, however, is just another way of saying that the demand is for the kind of intelligence which the specialist exhibits in his research work. The distinctive feature of research is precisely that it is not tied down to routine. It is constantly dealing with new situations requiring variations from routine. The well-trained research man is able to vary his procedure, because he can apply old principles to new situations, because he can make deductions so as to explain and predict. Vocational efficiency, therefore, requires emphasis on logical organization.

Teaching based on the theory of specific objectives does not provide such efficiency; nor, for that matter, does teaching based on the needs and interests of pupils. So we seem to be back to the teaching of the subject. Apparently the adventure into educational reform has miscarried.

Capacity for occupational readjustment in this modern age makes heavy demands both as to range and as to quality of educational equipment. The farmer of today affords a convenient illustration. He finds it useful to possess a wide acquaintance with the natural sciences, and he also finds himself drawn into questions of politics, finance, transportation, marketing, and all the rest. These matters are strictly continuous with his everyday occupation but the problems which he encounters are frequently new. They are not covered by what he may have learned in school. If education is to set him free, he must have the capacity to think independently after the manner of the specialist. An education based on specific objectives or on his interest in plants and farm animals would hardly serve the purpose when he is confronted with problems of crop control and farm relief.

But even this does not tell the whole story. We are all too familiar with the spectacle of the specialist who is astoundingly efficient in his own field and yet as helpless and as gullible as the rest of us outside of it. To set intelligence free obviously requires more than just a certain expertness within a relatively narrow area. Our farmer, for example, may be thoroughly scientific in his methods of fertilization and stock breeding and yet be entirely conventional in his notions concerning the function of government or his right to raise what he pleases and in any quantity that he can achieve. In holding to these conventional ideas he may be entirely right, but, if so, it is just a happy coincidence. These ideas, in his case, are not the product of "free intelligence;" they are inherited as absolute principles and are accepted as such. It appears, therefore, that intelligence cannot become free unless it faces the whole question of absolute versus relative standards. The challenge inherent in the Platonic tradition is a challenge to education all along the line. To meet this challenge is a basic and inescapable condition of freedom.

We Come Back to the Subjects

The foregoing discussion seems to warrant the conclusion that the contrast between teaching the child and teaching the subject is too simple to meet the requirements of the case. If we may assume that the purpose of teaching is to liberate the intelligence of the pupil, it appears that we must go into "logical organization" and beyond it. The pupil must acquire some capacity for thinking as the specialist thinks; and, in addition, he must see the bearing of the subject on the question of absolute standards. In the natural sciences, for example, he must come face to face with the question whether hypotheses and theories are merely "operational concepts" or whether they are to be taken as reliable accounts of eternal verities. Progressive education cannot fail to stress this issue without disloyalty to its basic and distinctive point of view. The contrast between child and subject, therefore, presents a false antithesis.

This is not to say that traditional education is to be given a clean bill of health. Its procedure, all too often, has been to transmit the organized results of science as something to be learned, without seeing to it that the concepts of science actually function for the organization of the experiences of the pupil as they function in the experience of the research specialist. One might say, therefore, that the teaching of science had nothing to do with science. And since this teaching took no account of the question of absolute standards, of what is really meant by evidence and truth, one is tempted to say that it had nothing to do with education either. It mistook technical proficiency for the cultivation of social insight or the improvement of the pupil's way of life. The dissatisfaction with this kind of thing is both understandable and justified.

This dissatisfaction, in progressive circles, took the form of revolt against "imposition" and "regimentation." Revolts, however, are negative. To raise a hue and cry against subjects is to pour out the baby with the bath. The traditional subjects stood for an educational value, which we neglect at our own peril. This value is directly related to the liberation of intelligence, for which progressive education assumes major responsibility. If intelligence is to become genuinely free, it must understand its own procedures, with reference to the "operational" character of concepts and with reference to the nature of evidence and truth. Subjects in the field of the natural sciences afford an invaluable opportunity for showing, both how "truth" is related to the way a new fact fits into the body of previous knowledge and how the organization of previous knowledge may be revised or reconstructed without assignable limit, not by any reference to absolutes, but solely in the interests of better control over experience. From the standpoint of the philosophy of progressive education, the opposition between absolutes and science is complete and irreconcilable. The fact that the traditional teaching of science has not revealed this opposition is nothing to the point.

If we neglect this clue we are once again out in Alice's Wonderland, where strange things come to pass. Our point of reference becomes something which is called "the whole child," or "self-activity," or the like. The pupil becomes his own standard of reference, which means that there is no standard at all. Tinkering in a laboratory becomes training in the scientific attitude, just as any splotching of colors and any flubdub in written composition can pass as creative self-expression. There is little ground for surprise that the more conservative members of the teaching profession view such innovations with scorn. Progressive education is again betrayed in its own household.

Freedom through Intelligence

When the individual pupil is thus isolated from his social context the concept of freedom likewise undergoes a curious distortion. In the philosophy of progressive education freedom becomes synonymous with the exercise of intelligence. The adult person who is hemmed in on all sides by bigotry and dogma is not free. Nor can a child be set free by the simple device of removing external restrictions. As William James told us many years ago, the young child is controlled by his environment; and this control, which "makes the child seem to belong less to himself than to every object which happens to catch his notice, is the first thing which a teacher must overcome. It is never overcome in some people, whose work, to the end of life, gets done in the interstices of their mind-wandering." [1] When the individual is detached from his surroundings, however, freedom is treated as if it were a kind of internal possession, requiring nothing but release from restrictions or controls. Advocates of such freedom are frequently under the erroneous impression that this is Dewey's conception of freedom. According to Dewey, freedom is achieved through the exercise of intelligence, whereas the less discriminating of his disciples understand him to mean that intelligence is achieved through the exercise of freedom.

Freedom through intelligence has its center in the ability to go through with an undertaking by the discovery of appropriate means, by the surmounting of obstacles, and by the modification of the original plan or conception in the light of new facts. This calls both for sustained effort in the presence of distractions, and for the exercise of discrimination and constructive imagination—in short, for real thinking. It may be added that, if we may trust the example of scientific thinking, the possession of a body of scientifically organized matter is of inestimable

[1] W. James, *Psychology*, Vol. I, p. 417.

value, not only as a resource in later life, but as a basis for present thinking. Where such subject matter is absent, we rely less on thinking than on guessing and more or less random experimenting. The lack of concern for the scientific organization of subject matter that is shown by the newer movements in education is an ominous fact. It tends to justify the suspicion that they seek to achieve the ends of education by a kind of magic.

In terms of Dewey's conception of freedom it is not at all evident that there is no place for compulsion or prescription. Any device is justified if it actually promotes thinking. Moreover, if adult psychology is any clue, it is conceivable that if children have a sense of responsibility and accountability they feel themselves sustained thereby. The pupil who inquired, "Do we have to do what we want to do today?", seems to have had a sense that something was lacking.

> Me this unchartered freedom tires;
> I feel the weight of chance desires.

Perhaps it is not irrelevant to mention that a number of the early Romanticists, after a period of dissipation in the exercise of "freedom," found an escape from the weight of chance desires by joining the Catholic Church. At any rate, it is not clear, either from the consideration of the underlying theory or from observation of the results of this type of education, that progressive education is finally on the right track.

The chief defect in American education today is the lack of a program, or sense of direction. It has no adequate mission or social gospel. Yet the material for a significant and distinctive educational philosophy is immediately at hand. The influence of modern science is pervading our whole civilization. It is giving us a new conception of the nature and method of intelligence and it is making the question of the place of intelligence in human affairs the fundamental issue of our civilization. To understand this issue is to have a basis for a philosophy of conduct and a basis for an interpretation of education in its relation to modern life.

CHAPTER VII

EDUCATION AS SOCIAL

It is agreed on all hands that education is a process of shaping or directing the development of the learner. Without such a conception of education there is no sense in trying to educate at all. The difficulty has been to decide on which basis or by which principle this business of shaping or directing is to be conducted. In its moments of weakness progressive education has turned for guiding principles to the individual child, and it is still doing so. Interests, needs, growth, the "whole child," and similar concepts have been offered as guiding principles. But in every case the light shed by these principles has turned out to be darkness.

PROGRESSIVE RECOGNITION OF SOCIAL EDUCATION

This emphasis on the learner, however, does not mean that the progressive movement has shown itself to be insensitive to the social character of education. On the contrary, the social has received an extraordinary amount of attention. It requires no high degree of discernment to see that the social environment exercises an overpowering influence on the development of the individual. The direction which comes from the social life by which he is surrounded is something to which every person is necessarily subjected.

As Kilpatrick says: "He cannot take part in that life on self-satisfying terms unless, for example, he learns to talk, both to understand and to make himself understood. Similarly he will, to be respectable in the eyes of his fellows, learn to manage the ordinary tools and forms of life. The urge to win approval will make many work assiduously to excel. This creates standards of respectability which the less ambitious will ignore only at the peril of their social standing. . . . The result is not an unmixed good, but the powerful effect is undeniable."[1]

Dewey speaks to the same point when he says: "The basic control resides in the nature of the situations in which the young take part. In social situations the young have to refer their way of acting to what others are doing and make it fit in. This directs their action to a common result, and gives an understanding common to the participants. For all

[1] Kilpatrick, *Remaking the Curriculum*, p. 54.

mean the same thing, even when performing different acts. This common understanding of the means and ends of action is the essence of social control." [2]

This participation in a common life is an essential condition for the enrichment of experience. A horse on a farm presumably does not see even the connection between his labor and his daily rations of feed; by human standards his life is intolerably dull and empty. By contrast the life of the farmer who uses the horse is incomparably richer, even under primitive conditions. There is a crop to be raised, a farm to be paid for, provision to be made for old age, a status in the community to be maintained; and on top of it all there is perhaps a sustaining sense that the Lord gives approval and rewards to industry and thrift. All these are social meanings, in the sense that they come to our farmer through his relations with others, and in the further sense that these meanings are valid for others as well. They embody a realm of realities, not Platonic but pragmatic, in which others live and operate as well as himself. Without such a context of meanings the farmer would be on approximately the same level as his horse.

[2] Dewey, *Democracy and Education*, p. 47.

On the principle that action and reaction are equal and opposite, it is perhaps not surprising that progressive education has at times shown a tendency to swing as far and as irresponsibly towards the social as, at other times, it has moved towards the individual. Since social relations count for so much, situations are set up in the school that call for co-operative effort and the sharing of experiences. Pupil planning, the group project, the socialized recitation, and other similar procedures are all, in one way or another, a recognition of the pervasive influence of social relations on the life of the individual. The attempt to exploit this influence for educational ends is commendable; the shortcomings of this attempt lie in the fact that no adequate criterion is furnished for distinguishing between desirable and undesirable social relations.

THE STANDARD FOR SOCIAL LIVING

What is meant by "social"? In one sense of the term a person is social if he shows a willingness to co-operate with others; in another sense he is social only if he works for good ends.

In the first sense every normal human being is incurably social, even without benefit of schooling.

As Dewey remarks: "There is honor among thieves, and a band of robbers has a common interest as respects its members. Gangs are marked by fraternal feeling, and narrow cliques by intense loyalty to their own codes. Family life may be marked by exclusiveness, suspicion, and jealousy as to those without, and yet be a model of amity and mutual aid within. Any education given by a group tends to socialize its members but the quality and value of the socialization depends upon the habits and aims of the group." [3]

We need a test of some kind. At this point there is a temptation to make the test a quantitative one. It may be said, for example, that such groups as those just cited show their antisocial character by their exclusiveness. Granted that these groups have a certain social quality within their respective organizations, they fall short of the requirements of true sociality in that they do not, or cannot, co-operate with others who are outside of the organization. The answer is that the "social" cannot be measured by any quantitative test. The gangster, or the bigot, cannot, indeed, co-operate with all comers but neither can the good man. If it is true that the criminal is out of step with good people,

3 Dewey, *op. cit.*, p. 95.

it is equally true that good people are out of step with the criminal. Good people have their own kind of exclusiveness. In Dewey's language, it is a matter of the "quality and value of the socialization," and not just a question of how much there is of it. Up to date, however, this point has not received a great deal of attention in progressive education.

If account is to be taken of the "quality and value of the socialization," some kind of standard is necessary. More specifically, if progressive education holds to democracy, it must have a standard for evaluating the democratic quality of social living. Such a standard Dewey finds in two tests, which are stated in interrogative form: "How numerous and varied are the interests which are consciously shared? How full and free is the interplay with other forms of association?" [4]

The attentive reader will note that this standard still places considerable emphasis on the quantitive side of the question. This makes it doubtful whether the standard is of much help in situations where help is most needed. How, for example, would this standard enable us to judge with respect to the relative merits of Nazi Germany and our own

[4] Dewey, *op. cit.*, p. 96.

United States? To make a count of the number
and variety of shared interests would get us no-
where. It is true that the Nazis do not share with
the Jews, but this has a certain offset in the fact
that Germany can co-operate with Italy to a much
greater extent than we should be able to do, to say
nothing of relations with Japan. Besides, Nazi
Germany is opening up new common interests for
itself, such as the development of a specifically German system of law and music and religion and the
high ambition to save the world from bolshevism.
Quantitative estimates are out of the question. Each
generalized attitude shuts out certain possibilities of
sharing and at the same time it creates its own distinctive opportunities for sharing. These new opportunities cannot be determined fully in advance;
they open up and grow with the course of events.
To attempt to decide among the respective merits
of competing ways of life on the basis of Dewey's
tests is, therefore, not a simple exercise in arithmetic
but a futile exercise of the imagination.

This is not to say, however, that the sharing of
interests and the co-operation which is a normal result of such sharing are not an essential consideration in determining the meaning of the social. As
was said earlier, the rise of the common man has

been the result of a struggle for participation in values or privileges which were denied to him. In this struggle the common man has frequently appealed to absolutes of his own, such as inalienable rights or natural law or what not. All of his legitimate claims are fully covered, however, by the principle that every man is entitled to the status of full membership in the life of the group. Negatively this means a rejection of special privilege, or the right of some people to get something for nothing. Positively it means participation in a world of common interests and purposes, which, in our previous illustration, marks the spiritual difference between the farmer and his horse. Democracy must take its clue from the idea of sharing.

In the past the common man has generally been more or less in the position of the horse, not because he was lacking in capacity, but because it was his misfortune to be the common man. It is the right of the common man to share in common interests, and, moreover, it is his right to share without having some outside authority define for him what these common interests are to be. No dictator, for example, can determine that these common interests must have their center in the idea of racial supremacy, as in the case of Nazi Germany. Our common man is entitled to have a share in deciding how the area of common interests is to grow.

The only principle to be observed here, if he is to remain loyal to the ideal of democracy, is that his activities must be of such a kind as to make for the continuous widening of the area of common interests and concerns. This is the only road leading to the maximum development of the individual. This principle gives us a criterion for distinguishing between good and bad forms of co-operative activity, i. e. of judging the "quality and value of socialization." We judge, not on the basis of the number and variety of interests held in common, but on the basis of the direction in which we are moving. In other words, we judge on the basis of the controlling ideal.

Given such a principle or standard, there is no difficulty whatever in distinguishing between Nazism and democracy. In the Nazi creed, the superiority of race is the final thing; which means that attention is deflected from continuously widening sharing to the exaltation or glorification of some one given interest. The moment this is done, the central interest is no longer the maximum development of the individual or "the more abundant life," but becomes something which tyrannizes over the individual. Blind obedience becomes a virtue, and the individual is expected to sacrifice willingly and without stint for a value which scarcely represents him at all.

DEMOCRACY A DISTINCTIVE WAY OF LIFE

It is clear that we have here another absolute. The principle of democracy, on the other hand, is not an absolute. In the first place, it is not an authoritative command from without, but an invitation to the individual to grow up to the full stature of his being. Secondly, since the principle of democracy rests on no other authority than the nature of the individual himself, it can never claim fixity or finality. The principle of democracy, represents, let us say, the best insight that we have, up to date, as to what is required for the fullest development of the individual. Whenever this insight is improved, our standard will vary accordingly.

The right kind of social living, then, possesses a certain "quality" or direction. It must not only conform to the requirements of democracy, but, if it is to have maximum effectiveness, it must be clearly conscious of its guiding principle. In terms of education, democracy·must be practiced in the everyday

affairs of the school, and, in addition, the way must
be opened for conscious loyalty to the principle of
democracy. The school has a distinctive obligation
to "intellectualize" this principle. It must make this
a direct aim or purpose.

Hence there is room for exceptions to Dewey's
view that "education as such has no aims. Only
persons, parents and teachers, etc., have aims, not an
abstract idea like education." [5] A statement like
this tends to confuse the issue. That abstractions
such as "education" have no aims must, of course,
be admitted. But, by the same reasoning, it might
be argued that the automobile industry has no aim
either. Aims are had only by persons like Ford and
Chrysler and the salesmen who follow us around.
The fact remains that the automobile industry is run
for a purpose quite different from that of a cotton
mill. If the principle of democracy needs to be in-
tellectualized, the school is the only institution which
we can expect to assume specific responsibility for it.

To intellectualize the principle of democracy it is
necessary, first of all, to rid ourselves of such superficial conceptions of democracy as the one expressed
in the following quotation: "If the people or their
representatives should vote to establish a censorship

[5] Dewey, *op. cit.*, p. 125.

of books or to prohibit smoking tobacco or to compel church attendance on Sunday, that would be democracy but it would not be a gain for freedom." [6] But the job is not done when we have presented a sound verbal statement of democracy in terms of purpose or direction. It must be understood in its bearings or implications, which means that it must be seen as a challenge to absolutes of whatever kind. There must be a realizing sense that belief in democracy may require a revision or reconstruction of beliefs and attitudes in every important domain of human interests. Democracy must stand revealed as a distinctive way of life and as a challenge to all the absolutes of history.

So we end where we began. Our clue to democracy lies in its quarrel with absolutes. Democracy stands for the common man and for the application of "operational" procedures in the construction of ideals or purposes, as well as in the determination of means for achieving predetermined goals. The great obstacle to democracy, down to the present day, is the Platonic philosophizing which lifts purposes or values out of the realm of everyday living and places them where "operational" procedures cannot reach them. The center of any

[6] E. D. Martin, *The Meaning of a Liberal Education*, p. 143.

educational program which professes to be democratic must be the irreconcilable conflict between democracy and absolutism.

IMPLICATIONS OF A SOCIAL IDEAL

It is the lack of an adequate social ideal that has burdened the progressive movement with a heavy load of trivialities and errors.

The innocent notion that promoting co-operative activities among pupils automatically prepares for citizenship in a democratic social order has obscured the fact that the remaking of outlook requires periods of solitude when the individual must wrestle himself. In extreme cases it has meant that everything must be done in committee, and so inevitably tended to produce a "herd mind" which remains pathetically dependent on group initiative and group opinion. Since the social as thus conceived provides no adequate guiding principle, the result was naturally that we were thrown back on interests and needs and the like for clues.

Nor are we any better off if we have recourse to "the whole child," unless we have a respectable notion of wholeness. If wholeness means, in Matthew Arnold's phrase, "to see life steadily and see it whole," the admonition to deal with "the whole child" becomes an appeal to direct the process of reconstructing experience toward those points where authoritarianism or absolutism comes into conflict with the implications of progressive education.

The philosophy of progressive education implies a challenging philosophy of social organization, as was stated at the beginning of our discussion (page 5) and has appeared in subsequent chapters. This implicit social ideal has been lost sight of, or has had only superficial consideration, by many exponents and adherents of the progressive movement. It remains to discuss further, in summary, the educational application of the democratic principle on which progressive education is properly based.

CHAPTER VIII

APPLYING THE PROGRESSIVE PHILOSOPHY

Since the emphasis on "wholeness" or "way of life," as described in the preceding chapters, has a direct bearing on the function of the school in a social order that professes allegiance to the principle of democracy, let us treat this relationship more specifically. No actual society is completely democratic in its practices. Absolutist beliefs and modes of thinking are far too deeply ingrained in our civilization to be laid aside very easily. Hence a special institution, such as the school, is now needed to cultivate the habit of relying on the foresight of consequences rather than on authority in the guidance of conduct. In other words, opportunity must be afforded for the practice of democracy.

If the consequences which are foreseen and which are made the controlling consideration relate to the continuous extension of shared interests and common purposes, the school becomes a place where democracy is applied to conduct. The conditions have then been especially devised or selected for the purpose of promoting habits of conduct in a democratic society and also insight into the meaning of democracy as a distinctive way of life.

This meaning of democracy naturally must be handled in terms of contrast with absolutism. To understand this meaning in generalized form undoubtedly requires a certain stage of chronological and intellectual maturity. Specific instances of the conflict between democracy and absolutism, however, are encountered at every level of the educative process. These will be exploited by the teacher who knows what he is about.

Superstitions in respect to natural phenomena or matters of health, for example, afford an opportunity for first steps toward the conception of science as the record of the long and painful process by which intelligence acquired the tools and the equipment for relying on itself rather than on authority. Bigotry and intolerance in respect to beliefs and customs appear in a different perspective when variations in such matters are related to differences in conditions and circumstances, and when account is taken of the requirements of democratic living. Given such a type of classroom work, the habits of living that are fostered by the school become reinforced by a growing intellectual insight into the meaning of democracy as an inclusive principle for the organization of personal and social life.

The teacher who is a specialist in a particular area of subject matter has at his disposal certain unique opportunities for relating this subject matter to the question of basic outlook or point of view. The history of the natural sciences, for example, is a record of a continuous struggle with time-hallowed tradition. Not only so, but the issue involved in this struggle was often misunderstood. It was frequently supposed that science was engaged in the business of building another extra-experiential world, made up of mechanical atoms and affording no room for human purposes and desires. This fictitious world was pictured as a huge, dead machine, which holds us in its remorseless grip. As a conception of reality it was considerably worse than that of Plato, and it called forth reactions of despair such as those expressed in James Thomson's *City of Dreadful Night* and W. E. Henley's *Invictus*. In most cases, however, an escape from pessimism was found by retaining a world of supernaturalism alongside of the naturalistic scheme of modern science. This combination presents a highly unstable state of equilibrium; and it has the unfortunate result of preventing the learner from acquiring a realizing sense of the fact that science affords the possibility of placing man squarely in the center of the picture. If we treat scientific ideas as "operational concepts," we are no longer compelled to choose between pessimism and the belief in an extra-experiential realm which provides sanctions for human values.

In the social sciences the situation presents a certain parallel to that of the natural sciences. Here again we find a record of continuous conflict and struggle. With changing conditions and growth in racial experience and knowledge, new interests and values tend to emerge and to seek embodiment in customs, institutions, and practices. In so doing they naturally impinge on older ways of living and thus tend to produce conflict. These older ways are normally entrenched behind an array of absolutes, in the form of customs, traditional modes of thinking, and supernatural sanctions; so they are very likely to offer stiff resistance. As a rule, however, the conflict is not interpreted in terms of absolutism versus democracy, but as a conflict among absolutes. In the end we accept the new values pretty much as we have accepted the naturalism of science, without achieving any very satisfactory integration of the new values with the old.

Since the medieval period, for example, the ecclesiastical point of view has adjusted itself to a worldly ideal of "classical" literary education; it has accepted science as a major cultural value, and it has accorded to industry and finance a status of eminent respectability.[1] The net result of all this is that the average modern man, whether educated or not, lives in a state of incredible mental confusion. He has no point of view, but merely points of view, which get into one another's way and prevent the development of an effective way of life.

The history of our own country is a case in point. The ideal of democracy was developed under conditions vastly different from those which prevail at the present time. Democracy was, in the main, a political concept with a simple content. With changes in conditions new meanings and new values appeared, which, however, did not entirely displace the old meanings. As a consequence, democracy has become an ideal in which we still believe but which we no longer understand.[2]

When some one value or set of values is arbitrarily selected as final and absolute, we have the principle of dictatorship. The alternative is a policy for the

[1] W. H. Kilpatrick, *The Educational Frontier*, Chapter I.
[2] B. H. Bode, *Democracy as a Way of Life*.

continuous extension of common interests, which does not give preferred status to any specific value or prescribe what people are to believe. In a word, the primary obligation in the teaching of the social sciences is to make clear the intellectual confusion which has overtaken the modern world, and to deal with this confusion in its relation to the need for regaining a unified and consistent way of life.

In literature and art we again encounter the ubiquitous question of absolutes. Traditionally we have leaned to the view that there are absolute standards of beauty. These standards were determined by the test of "universality," by which was meant prevalence over long periods of time and among different classes of people. In education this led to the practice of selecting certain classics for classroom material and then endeavoring by all possible means to cultivate liking or appreciation for them.

The rejection of absolute standards calls for a different approach. All art then takes on an "operational" character. That is, art is a way of enhancing appreciation through the media of form, line, or tone. More concisely, art enhances appreciation through *artifice*. The teaching of art, therefore, starts appropriately with appreciations which the learner already possesses; and it seeks to lead him to the discovery that these appreciations can be heightened by the devices or "artifices" which are peculiar to art.[3] It follows at once, of course, that art is a relative thing.

It also follows that art can serve as a powerful reinforcement of the teaching in other fields. In the end all teaching must secure appreciation or fail of its purpose. The conflicts and struggles, for example, to which reference was made in the foregoing paragraphs, must become living values in the experience of the learner, if education is not to degenerate into a clever manipulation of intellectual symbols. The things of continuing value that men have sacrificed and fought for and the emerging ideals of our civilization must be clothed with the flesh and blood of reality. To secure a "realizing sense" on the part of the learner is frequently no easy task. Education can scarcely hope to achieve its ends without the support of art. There is a sense, therefore, in which art represents the final embodiment of educational values.

These are, of course, merely sketchy indications of the direction in which we must go. The important thing is to realize that progressive education carries within itself the organizing principle for a whole

[3] Cf. John Dewey, *Art as Experience*, Chapter I.

way of life. It should be evident that there is no warrant whatsoever for any smug complacency, as though the basic problems of education were all settled, when, in fact, we are just beginning to sense what they are. Progressive education has a unique opportunity to become an avowed exponent of a democratic philosophy of life, which is the last remaining hope that the common man will eventually come into his own.

INDEX

AMERICAN EDUCATION:
ITS MEN, IDEAS, AND INSTITUTIONS
An Arno Press/New York Times Collection

Series I

Adams, Francis. **The Free School System of the United States.** 1875.

Alcott, William A. **Confessions of a School Master.** 1839.

American Unitarian Association. **From Servitude to Service.** 1905.

Bagley, William C. **Determinism in Education.** 1925.

Barnard, Henry, editor. **Memoirs of Teachers, Educators, and Promoters and Benefactors of Education, Literature, and Science.** 1861.

Bell, Sadie. **The Church, the State, and Education in Virginia.** 1930.

Belting, Paul Everett. **The Development of the Free Public High School in Illinois to 1860.** 1919.

Berkson, Isaac B. **Theories of Americanization: A Critical Study.** 1920.

Blauch, Lloyd E. **Federal Cooperation in Agricultural Extension Work, Vocational Education, and Vocational Rehabilitation.** 1935.

Bloomfield, Meyer. **Vocational Guidance of Youth.** 1911.

Brewer, Clifton Hartwell. **A History of Religious Education in the Episcopal Church to 1835.** 1924.

Brown, Elmer Ellsworth. **The Making of Our Middle Schools.** 1902.

Brumbaugh, M. G. **Life and Works of Christopher Dock.** 1908.

Burns, Reverend J. A. **The Catholic School System in the United States.** 1908.

Burns, Reverend J. A. **The Growth and Development of the Catholic School System in the United States.** 1912.

Burton, Warren. **The District School as It Was.** 1850.

Butler, Nicholas Murray, editor. **Education in the United States.** 1900.

Butler, Vera M. **Education as Revealed By New England Newspapers prior to 1850.** 1935.

Campbell, Thomas Monroe. **The Movable School Goes to the Negro Farmer.** 1936.

Carter, James G. **Essays upon Popular Education.** 1826.

Carter, James G. **Letters to the Hon. William Prescott, LL.D., on the Free Schools of New England.** 1824.

Channing, William Ellery. **Self-Culture.** 1842.

Coe, George A. **A Social Theory of Religious Education.** 1917.

Committee on Secondary School Studies. **Report of the Committee on Secondary School Studies, Appointed at the Meeting of the National Education Association.** 1893.

✓ Counts, George S. **Dare the School Build a New Social Order?** 1932.

Counts, George S. **The Selective Character of American Secondary Education.** 1922.

Counts, George S. **The Social Composition of Boards of Education.** 1927.

Culver, Raymond B. **Horace Mann and Religion in the Massachusetts Public Schools.** 1929.

Curoe, Philip R. V. **Educational Attitudes and Policies of Organized Labor in the United States.** 1926.

Dabney, Charles William. **Universal Education in the South.** 1936.

Dearborn, Ned Harland. **The Oswego Movement in American Education.** 1925.

De Lima, Agnes. **Our Enemy the Child.** 1926.

Dewey, John. **The Educational Situation.** 1902.

Dexter, Franklin B., editor. **Documentary History of Yale University.** 1916.

Eliot, Charles William. **Educational Reform: Essays and Addresses.** 1898.

Ensign, Forest Chester. **Compulsory School Attendance and Child Labor.** 1921.

Fitzpatrick, Edward Augustus. **The Educational Views and Influence of De Witt Clinton.** 1911.

Fleming, Sanford. **Children & Puritanism.** 1933.

Flexner, Abraham. **The American College: A Criticism.** 1908.

Foerster, Norman. **The Future of the Liberal College.** 1938.

Gilman, Daniel Coit. **University Problems in the United States.** 1898.

Hall, Samuel R. **Lectures on School-Keeping.** 1829.

Hall, Stanley G. **Adolescence: Its Psychology and Its Relations to Physiology, Anthropology, Sociology, Sex, Crime, Religion, and Education.** 1905. 2 vols.

Hansen, Allen Oscar. **Early Educational Leadership in the Ohio Valley.** 1923.

Harris, William T. **Psychologic Foundations of Education.** 1899.

Harris, William T. **Report of the Committee of Fifteen on the Elementary School.** 1895.

Harveson, Mae Elizabeth. **Catharine Esther Beecher: Pioneer Educator.** 1932.

Jackson, George Leroy. **The Development of School Support in Colonial Massachusetts.** 1909.

Kandel, I. L., editor. **Twenty-five Years of American Education.** 1924.

Kemp, William Webb. **The Support of Schools in Colonial New York by the Society for the Propagation of the Gospel in Foreign Parts.** 1913.

Kilpatrick, William Heard. **The Dutch Schools of New Netherland and Colonial New York.** 1912.

Kilpatrick, William Heard. **The Educational Frontier.** 1933.

Knight, Edgar Wallace. **The Influence of Reconstruction on Education in the South.** 1913.

Le Duc, Thomas. **Piety and Intellect at Amherst College, 1865-1912.** 1946.

Maclean, John. **History of the College of New Jersey from Its Origin in 1746 to the Commencement of 1854.** 1877.

Maddox, William Arthur. **The Free School Idea in Virginia before the Civil War.** 1918.

Mann, Horace. **Lectures on Education.** 1855.

McCadden, Joseph J. **Education in Pennsylvania, 1801-1835, and Its Debt to Roberts Vaux.** 1855.

McCallum, James Dow. **Eleazar Wheelock.** 1939.

McCuskey, Dorothy. **Bronson Alcott, Teacher.** 1940.

Meiklejohn, Alexander. **The Liberal College.** 1920.

Miller, Edward Alanson. **The History of Educational Legislation in Ohio from 1803 to 1850.** 1918.

Miller, George Frederick. **The Academy System of the State of New York.** 1922.

Monroe, Will S. **History of the Pestalozzian Movement in the United States.** 1907.

Mosely Education Commission. **Reports of the Mosely Education Commission to the United States of America October-December, 1903.** 1904.

Mowry, William A. **Recollections of a New England Educator.** 1908.

Mulhern, James. **A History of Secondary Education in Pennsylvania.** 1933.

National Herbart Society. **National Herbart Society Yearbooks 1-5, 1895-1899.** 1895-1899.

Nearing, Scott. **The New Education: A Review of Progressive Educational Movements of the Day.** 1915.

Neef, Joseph. **Sketches of a Plan and Method of Education.** 1808.

Nock, Albert Jay. **The Theory of Education in the United States.** 1932.

Norton, A. O., editor. **The First State Normal School in America: The Journals of Cyrus Pierce and Mary Swift.** 1926.

Oviatt, Edwin. **The Beginnings of Yale, 1701-1726.** 1916.

Packard, Frederic Adolphus. **The Daily Public School in the United States.** 1866.

Page, David P. **Theory and Practice of Teaching.** 1848.

Parker, Francis W. **Talks on Pedagogics: An Outline of the Theory of Concentration.** 1894.

Peabody, Elizabeth Palmer. **Record of a School.** 1835.

Porter, Noah. **The American Colleges and the American Public.** 1870.

Reigart, John Franklin. **The Lancasterian System of Instruction in the Schools of New York City.** 1916.

Reilly, Daniel F. **The School Controversy (1891-1893).** 1943.

Rice, Dr. J. M. **The Public-School System of the United States.** 1893.

Rice, Dr. J. M. **Scientific Management in Education.** 1912.

Ross, Early D. **Democracy's College: The Land-Grant Movement in the Formative Stage.** 1942.

Rugg, Harold, et al. **Curriculum-Making: Past and Present.** 1926.

Rugg, Harold, et al. **The Foundations of Curriculum-Making.** 1926.

Rugg, Harold and Shumaker, Ann. **The Child-Centered School.** 1928.

Seybolt, Robert Francis. **Apprenticeship and Apprenticeship Education in Colonial New England and New York.** 1917.

Seybolt, Robert Francis. **The Private Schools of Colonial Boston.** 1935.

Seybolt, Robert Francis. **The Public Schools of Colonial Boston.** 1935.

Sheldon, Henry D. **Student Life and Customs.** 1901.

Sherrill, Lewis Joseph. **Presbyterian Parochial Schools, 1846-1870.** 1932 .

Siljestrom, P. A. **Educational Institutions of the United States.** 1853.

Small, Walter Herbert. **Early New England Schools.** 1914.

Soltes, Mordecai. **The Yiddish Press: An Americanizing Agency.** 1925.

Stewart, George, Jr. **A History of Religious Education in Connecticut to the Middle of the Nineteenth Century.** 1924.

Storr, Richard J. **The Beginnings of Graduate Education in America.** 1953.

Stout, John Elbert. **The Development of High-School Curricula in the North Central States from 1860 to 1918.** 1921.

Suzzallo, Henry. **The Rise of Local School Supervision in Massachusetts.** 1906.

Swett, John. **Public Education in California.** 1911.

Tappan, Henry P. **University Education.** 1851.

Taylor, Howard Cromwell. **The Educational Significance of the Early Federal Land Ordinances.** 1921.

Taylor, J. Orville. **The District School.** 1834.

Tewksbury, Donald G. **The Founding of American Colleges and Universities before the Civil War.** 1932.

Thorndike, Edward L. **Educational Psychology.** 1913-1914.

True, Alfred Charles. **A History of Agricultural Education in the United States, 1785-1925.** 1929.

True, Alfred Charles. **A History of Agricultural Extension Work in the United States, 1785-1923.** 1928.

Updegraff, Harlan. **The Origin of the Moving School in Massachusetts.** 1908.

Wayland, Francis. **Thoughts on the Present Collegiate System in the United States.** 1842.

Weber, Samuel Edwin. **The Charity School Movement in Colonial Pennsylvania.** 1905.

Wells, Guy Fred. **Parish Education in Colonial Virginia.** 1923.

Wickersham, J. P. **The History of Education in Pennsylvania.** 1885.

Woodward, Calvin M. **The Manual Training School.** 1887.

Woody, Thomas. **Early Quaker Education in Pennsylvania.** 1920.

Woody, Thomas. **Quaker Education in the Colony and State of New Jersey.** 1923.

Wroth, Lawrence C. **An American Bookshelf, 1755.** 1934.

Series II

Adams, Evelyn C. **American Indian Education.** 1946.

Bailey, Joseph Cannon. **Seaman A. Knapp: Schoolmaster of American Agriculture.** 1945.

Beecher, Catharine and Harriet Beecher Stowe. **The American Woman's Home.** 1869.

Benezet, Louis T. **General Education in the Progressive College.** 1943.

Boas, Louise Schutz. **Woman's Education Begins.** 1935.

Bobbitt, Franklin. **The Curriculum.** 1918.

Bode, Boyd H. **Progressive Education at the Crossroads.** 1938.

Bourne, William Oland. **History of the Public School Society of the City of New York.** 1870.

Bronson, Walter C. **The History of Brown University, 1764-1914.** 1914.

Burstall, Sara A. **The Education of Girls in the United States.** 1894.

Butts, R. Freeman. **The College Charts Its Course.** 1939.

Caldwell, Otis W. and Stuart A. Courtis. **Then & Now in Education, 1845-1923.** 1923.

Calverton, V. F. & Samuel D. Schmalhausen, editors. **The New Generation: The Intimate Problems of Modern Parents and Children.** 1930.

Charters, W. W. **Curriculum Construction.** 1923.

Childs, John L. **Education and Morals.** 1950.

Childs, John L. Education and the Philosophy of Experimentalism. 1931.

Clapp, Elsie Ripley. Community Schools in Action. 1939.

Counts, George S. The American Road to Culture: A Social Interpretation of Education in the United States. 1930.

Counts, George S. School and Society in Chicago. 1928.

Finegan, Thomas E. Free Schools. 1921.

Fletcher, Robert Samuel. A History of Oberlin College. 1943.

Grattan, C. Hartley. In Quest of Knowledge: A Historical Perspective on Adult Education. 1955.

Hartman, Gertrude & Ann Shumaker, editors. Creative Expression. 1932.

Kandel, I. L. The Cult of Uncertainty. 1943.

Kandel, I. L. Examinations and Their Substitutes in the United States. 1936.

Kilpatrick, William Heard. Education for a Changing Civilization. 1926.

Kilpatrick, William Heard. Foundations of Method. 1925.

Kilpatrick, William Heard. The Montessori System Examined. 1914.

Lang, Ossian H., editor. Educational Creeds of the Nineteenth Century. 1898.

Learned, William S. The Quality of the Educational Process in the United States and in Europe. 1927.

Meiklejohn, Alexander. The Experimental College. 1932.

Middlekauff, Robert. Ancients and Axioms: Secondary Education in Eighteenth-Century New England. 1963.

Norwood, William Frederick. Medical Education in the United States Before the Civil War. 1944.

Parsons, Elsie W. Clews. Educational Legislation and Administration of the Colonial Governments. 1899.

Perry, Charles M. Henry Philip Tappan: Philosopher and University President. 1933.

Pierce, Bessie Louise. Civic Attitudes in American School Textbooks. 1930.

Rice, Edwin Wilbur. The Sunday-School Movement (1780-1917) and the American Sunday-School Union (1817-1917). 1917.

Robinson, James Harvey. The Humanizing of Knowledge. 1924.

Ryan, W. Carson. Studies in Early Graduate Education. 1939.

Seybolt, Robert Francis. The Evening School in Colonial America. 1925.

Seybolt, Robert Francis. Source Studies in American Colonial Education. 1925.

Todd, Lewis Paul. Wartime Relations of the Federal Government and the Public Schools, 1917-1918. 1945.

Vandewalker, Nina C. The Kindergarten in American Education. 1908.

Ward, Florence Elizabeth. The Montessori Method and the American School. 1913.

West, Andrew Fleming. Short Papers on American Liberal Education. 1907.

Wright, Marion M. Thompson. The Education of Negroes in New Jersey. 1941.

Supplement

The Social Frontier (Frontiers of Democracy). Vols. 1-10, 1934-1943.